Empire in the East
The Story of
Genghis Khan

Empire in the East
The Story of
Genghis Khan

Earle Rice Jr.

MORGAN
REYNOLDS
PUBLISHING
Greensboro, North Carolina

WORLD LEADERS

GEORGE C. MARSHALL
ADOLF HITLER
WOODROW WILSON
VACLAV HAVEL
GENGHIS KHAN
JOSEPH STALIN
CHE GUEVARA

EMPIRE IN THE EAST: THE STORY OF GENGHIS KHAN

Library of Congress Cataloging-in-Publication Data

Rice, Earle.
    Empire in the east: the story of Genghis Khan / Earle Rice, Jr.— 1st ed.
      p. cm.
  Audience: Ages 10+
Includes bibliographical references and index.
    ISBN 13: 978-1-931798-62-4
    ISBN 10: 1-931798-62-1
1. Genghis Khan, 1162-1227—Juvenile literature. 2. Mongols—Kings and
rulers—Biography—Juvenile literature. I. Title: Story of Genghis Khan. II.
Title.
    DS22.R53 2005
    950'.21'092—dc22

                  2004030743

Printed in the United States of America
First Edition

Contents

A Note on Sources

The story of Genghis Khan has captured imaginations ever since he first took control of the Mongol people. But because he lived in a preliterate society, the details of his life were not recorded as they unfolded.

The main source of information about Genghis Khan is a mysterious and cryptic document called *The Secret History of the Mongols* that was probably penned within twenty years of his death. Many attribute authorship to Shigi-Khutukhu, one of the khan's adopted brothers.

The document was long considered lost until a copy was uncovered in the nineteenth century. Unfortunately, this copy was written in Chinese characters organized in a code intended to phonetically represent the Mongolian language of the thirteenth century. Work on the translation was hampered by the interference of the Soviet Communist government, which feared that the legendary document would inspire nationalistic fervor among the Mongols. But by the 1980s, translations in English began to appear, and with the collapse of Soviet Communism in 1990, a resurgence of interest in and study of Genghis Khan began.

His is a story still shrouded in mystery. Because so little concrete information was available, the khan's legend grew over the centuries, eventually coming to include wild and fanciful tales. Though it is difficult to separate fact from fiction eight hundred years later, most scholars have concluded that *The Secret History of the Mongols*, which has been translated into various forms, is a remarkably accurate depiction of this legendary man and the dramatic world he inhabited.

Vast Lands, Scattered People

Yesugei Ba'atur (Yesugei the Brave) was out hunting one morning along the banks of the Onon River in northeastern Mongolia, when he spotted a young man on horseback trotting alongside a woman riding in a cart. Reining in his pony, Yesugei observed the couple from a distance. From his manner of dress and his hairstyle, he could tell the young man was a nobleman of the Merkid tribe. The woman, he later learned, was a member of the Olkhunuud tribe, and the two were newlyweds. Yesugei made careful note of the couple's slow pace and the loneliness of the steppes, then headed back to camp.

In the twelfth century, Mongols customarily married outside their own tribes, and it was therefore common for men to travel great distances to seek wives. Prospec-

Opposite: Genghis Khan. *(Bibliothèque nationale de France, Paris)*

Yesugei catches his first glimpse of Hoelun as she passes him in a cart with her new husband.

tive grooms were expected to pay a hefty price for their brides, and often worked for the woman's family for several years before returning to their own tribes—a period known as bride service. Here, Yesugei saw an easy opportunity to circumvent this time- and labor-intensive process.

Back in camp, Yesugei asked two of his brothers to mount their horses. Men of the steppes rarely refused a call for help from a family member, lest calls of their own go unanswered in some future time of need. Within a few hours, the brothers had captured the woman, Hoelun, and driven off her husband. Yesugei claimed her as his new wife, triumphantly bringing her and her few possessions back to camp.

In one morning, Hoelun had lost one husband and gained another. That afternoon, she was introduced to her new family: Yesugei's other wife, Sochigel, and their two sons, Begter and Belgutei.

At this time, the custom on the steppes permitted a man to marry as many wives as he could support, but only one wife—his chief or principal wife—could bear his heirs. Given the widespread impoverishment of the nomads, few men could afford more than one wife. As the leader of his small tribe, Yesugei had enough power and influence to keep two wives, and to house them in separate *gers,* which contributed to more harmonious familial relations. *Ger* is a Mongolian term for a round, portable tent built on a light wicker frame and covered in felt. But Yesugei's tribe was by no means wealthy, subsisting mainly on the small animals it hunted along the wooded northern fringes of the steppes.

Despite her challenging circumstances, Hoelun proved herself to be strong and resourceful. She quickly

This image, from Persian historian Rashid al-Din's *Jami al-Tawarikh (World History),* completed in 1314, portrays a typical Mongol camp, complete with *gers.* *(Bibliothèque nationale de France, Paris)*

established herself as Yesugei's principal wife and, in 1162, gave birth to her first child, a son. Just before the boy was born, Yesugei had returned from a successful battle in which he captured two Tatar princes, Temujin Uge and Khori Buka. It was the custom on the steppes to name a child in commemoration of an important event at the time of his birth. Thus the baby boy was called Temujin, after the mightier of the recently captured princes. In Mongolian, the name means "ironworker" or "blacksmith" or, by extension, "man of iron."

The world would come to know Temujin by another name, and by that name he would one day gain fame and notoriety as the most feared conqueror to ever walk the Earth—Genghis Khan.

Young Temujin had to survive a difficult and often dangerous childhood. In the twelfth century, the steppes of Mongolia were a wild and lonely place, inhabited by bands of people who hunted or farmed or otherwise eked out a living in one of the most barren but beautiful places on Earth.

These images depict two myths of the origin of Genghis Khan. One shows him decended from a gray-blue wolf. The other portrays a celestial light that fertilized Alan Qo'a, an ancestral mother of the khans. *(Museum of Inner Mongolia)*

The tribes of Mongolia had once been a united and powerful people under the leadership of Khabul Khan ("khan" is an honorific meaning "chief" or "king") and his ancestors. Early in the twelfth century, Khabul Khan died under mysterious circumstances. His followers suspected he had been poisoned, possibly by agents of the Chinese emperor whom he had recently offended. Almost twenty-five years of war between the Mongols and the Chinese followed.

The Mongols elected a man called Ambakhai to succeed Khabul Khan. While struggling against the Chinese, Ambakhai's people also faced attacks from the Tatars, their nomad neighbors to the south.

In an effort to improve relations, Ambakhai offered his daughter in marriage to a Tatar prince. En route to consummate the marriage agreement, a group of different Tatars swooped down on the khan's party, captured Ambakhai, and sent him off to the Chinese emperor, who sentenced him to death. Before he was killed, Ambakhai sent a message home. He requested that it be delivered to Khabul's son Khutula and to Kaidan, one of his own sons. The message was simple: it asked them to spend the rest of their lives avenging his death.

Ambakhai Khan was nailed to a wooden ass, flayed alive, and then chopped to pieces, starting with his fingers and toes and proceeding slowly until his whole body was reduced to bits. A hundred years later, Mongols would still remember these words of Ambakhai Khan, and in their heed would slaughter countless Tatars and Chinese.

The Mongols called for a *khuriltai* (official council or meeting) on the wooded banks of the Khorkhonag River where it joins the Onon. They elected Khutula as Ambakhai's successor, partly because he was one of the two men to whom the unfortunate khan had sent his last message.

The Mongols celebrated Khutula's election with food and drink and dancing, for they felt certain that he would restore them to the glory days under Khabul. Legend has it that men danced around the council fires until the dust they formed reached their knees, and around nearby trees until their dancing feet stomped waist-deep furrows.

Under Khutula, the Mongols enjoyed a temporary resurgence on the battlefield. They inflicted heavy losses on the Chinese and returned home laden with spoils. But their successes against the Chinese did not carry over against the Tatars, who came thundering down upon them from the south and east, scattering Mongol clans, slaying the people, and driving off the cattle and horses from their pastures around demolished camps. Under Khutula, the Mongols fought thirteen major battles with the Tatars and lost thirteen times. At the start of the 1160s, the Mongol empire collapsed, and Khutula Khan took his place in history as the last khan of all the Mongols.

The Tatars did not annihilate the Mongols totally but reduced their ranks by a great number and sent them fleeing into the forests or across the vast steppes. Plenty of the Mongols survived but in disorganized groups.

Among the Mongol leaders who survived the Tatar wars was Bartan Ba'atur, son of Khabul Khan and elder brother of Khutula. Although Bartan had been passed over as khan in favor of his brother, the title Ba'atur meant that he was a powerful, noble warrior and a strong prince.

After the breakup of the Mongol empire, feuds between rival tribes became commonplace. Bartan Ba'atur was killed in one such fight, and his son, Yesugei, inherited the leadership of their clan. Now he had a son and heir, young Temujin.

In the age of Yesugei Ba'atur, men stood an even chance of starving or freezing to death or dying in violent conflict on the harsh plains of the Mongolian Plateau. The plateau forms a part of the vast expanse of open lands known as the steppes, which extend across the breadth of central Asia from Manchuria in the east to Hungary in the west. Natural barriers isolated the inhabitants of the plateau and sheltered them from outside intrusion for centuries. In the west, two great mountain chains, the Altai and the Tian Shan, converge to obstruct any approach to the plateau. The Khingan Mountains prevent access from the east and north, and vast frozen Siberian forests—clasped in the fingers of still more mountains: the Sayan, Yablonovy, and Hentiyn—stand like endless pickets in a fence to fend off potential invaders. The south is bounded by the treacherous and unforgiving Gobi desert.

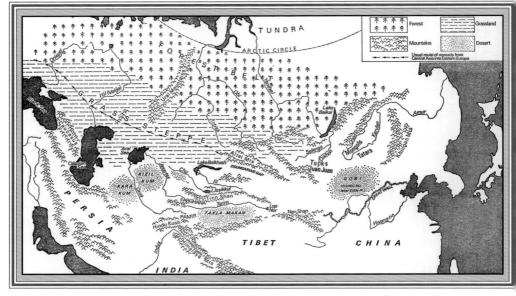

The lands and terrain of the nomadic peoples of Asia at the time of Temujin's birth.

Three principal river systems originate in the mountains on three sides of the plateau. From the eastern mountains, the Kerulen, the Khailar, and the Kan flow down into the Argun River; the Onon and the Ingoda join the Shilka River; and the Argun and the Shilka in turn feed the distant Amur River as it winds to the far-off Sea of Okhotsk. Out of the central heights, the Tuul, Orhon, and Khilok empty into the Salenga River as it courses northward to Lake Baikal. And from the western peaks rise the streams that form the Arctic-bound Siberian rivers—the Yenisei, the Ob, and the Irtysh.

The Mongolian Plateau stands some 4,000 feet (1,200 meters) above sea level, and dramatic extremes of climate are common. Temperatures often soar above 104° F (40° C) in the summer and plummet well below –40° F (–40° C) in the winter. Notwithstanding its river systems, most of the land on the plateau is unsuitable for farming. The actual soil varies from a loose gravel to a thin clay and freezes solidly during the winter. Streams, rivers, and lakes also freeze from November until April. The severe climate, poor soil quality, and low rainfall add up to something less than an agricultural paradise.

"The land is only in the hundredth part fruitful and cannot support crops unless irrigated," wrote Brother John of Plano Carpini, of the Order of Friars Minor, "however water and streams there are few and the rivers are rare." The Italian friar served as Pope Innocent IV's envoy to the Mongols and became the first European to enter this land in 1245. He reported further, "The weather there is extremely variable. In fact, in the middle of summer, when other areas usually have the greatest heat, there is a good deal of thunder and lightning which kills many people, and a great deal of snow falls there then. There are great cold windstorms too, so that often men can ride horses only with difficulty. . . . In winter it never rains there, while in summer it often does, but so little that it can hardly soak the dust and roots of the pasture. Hail, by contrast, falls abundantly. . . . And in the summer there may suddenly be extreme heat and then suddenly extreme cold. During the winter in one area a very great deal of snow falls, while in another very little."

The Mongolian Plateau consists of three distinct and separate sectors: the mountainous wooded region in the north, the open grasslands in the center, and the barren desert lands in the south. The land now known as

The Mongols were known for their excellent hunting skills. This Persian image from 1300 shows two horsemen feasting on their catch.

Mongolia occupies the easternmost part of the steppes. Various tribes—such as the Turks, the Mongols, and the Tungus—have peopled the plateau for untold centuries. To varying degrees, they have common characteristics in legend, written history, kinship, and particularly language, as they belonged to the Altaic linguistic community (named for the Altai Mountains).

In Yesugei's time, few people chose to live in the desert. The Mongol heartland was centered at the headwaters of the Onon, Kerulen, and Tuul Rivers around the holy mountain Burkhan Khaldun. Yesugei's people were herder-hunters who tended small flocks at the northern edge of the steppes and combed the deep forests of fir, larch, birch, and aspen in search of all kinds of wild-life—elks, bears, boars, wolves, foxes, wild sheep, sables, otters, rabbits, and more. In addition to meat, leather, and fur, the animals also provided antlers, horns, tusks, teeth, and bones that the Mongols used for fashioning assorted tools, weapons, and ornaments. The hunter tribes rarely strayed beyond Lake Baikal, whereas the pastoral tribes to the south roamed across the broad reaches of the steppes from the foothills of the Altai Mountains in the west to Buir Nor in the east.

In the middle of the twelfth century, the Mongols were one of a number of small nomadic tribes that inhabited the plateau. The two most important tribes were the Kereyid and the Naiman. The Kereyid, who were thought to be of Turkish origin, lived in the center of the plateau along the rich pasturelands of the Orhon and Tuul Rivers, while the Naiman homeland lay west of the Kereyid in the Altai Mountains. Their neighbors to the south were the Uighurs, another Turkic tribe that became the first seminomadic tribe to gain literacy.

Life on the steppes demanded an endless cycle of seasonal migrations from the open pasturelands in the summer to the sheltered river valleys in the winter. Three animals occupied a prominent place in this lifestyle: sheep, cattle, and horses. Sheep provided the main staples of life: meat, milk, and cheese for nourishment, and leather and wool for clothing and making felt for *gers*. In the autumn, each Mongol family slaughtered a number of its sheep, prepared the mutton, and froze it, usually by burying it before the first snows. Later, the family cooked it by melting a large block of ice in a kettle and boiling frozen slabs of the meat until it formed a thick stew. This store of protein-rich frozen mutton helped to sustain the family through the long winter. Cattle and horses also provided a source of some meat, but the Mongols primarily used cattle as draft animals and horses for transportation, tending herds, hunting, and fighting. The fermented milk of mares produced another staple of Mongol fare known as *airak*, a slightly bitter and mildly alcoholic drink.

During a typical family meal, the seating arrangement in the family *ger* favored the adult warriors and guests, who sat nearest to the fire in the center beneath the smoke hole in the top of the felt tent. Women sat a little back on the left side, and children fit in wherever they could find space. All their food was cooked in a community pot and eaten from it. The pot went first to the men, then to the aged and the women, and finally to the children. After everyone had eaten, there was rarely enough left for the family dog to grow fat on.

In the spring and summer when game was most plentiful, the Mongols ate fairly well, but during the frigid months when game was less available, they would eat anything edible. The Italian friar, John of Plano Carpini, noted: "They regard anything which can be eaten as food: they eat dogs, wolves, foxes and horses, and, when in difficulty, they eat human flesh. Thus, when they attacked a particular Chinese city, and their emperor

This image of a Mongol man crouching over the dinner pot was painted by the Turkish artist Mehmet Siyah Kalem in the fifteenth century. *(Museum of Inner Mongolia)*

himself conducted the siege, they found after they had besieged it a long while that the Tartars [Mongols] had used up all their supplies and did not have enough for all the men to eat, so they took one of every ten men to eat. . . . Furthermore, we saw them eat lice. . . . We actually saw them eat mice."

An obscure thirteenth-century author named C. de Bridia (his first name is not known) wrote an account of the Mongols entitled *Historia Tartarorum*—better known as *The Tartar Relation*—based on the accounts of Plano Carpini and other friars in his expedition. (Western Europeans often referred to the Mongols as Tartars, either out of confusion with the neighboring tribe of

Tatars, or as a way of collectively relating the fearsome Asian tribes to Tartarus, a hellish underworld in Greek mythology.) C. de Bridia offered this description of the Mongols:

> Tartars are generally of low stature and rather thin, owing to their diet of mare's milk, which makes a man thin, and their strenuous life. They are broad of face with prominent cheekbones, and have a tonsure [shaven crown] on their heads like our clerics from which they shave a strip three fingers wide from ear to ear. On the forehead, however, they wear their hair in a crescent-shaped fringe reaching to the eyebrows, but gather up the remaining hair, and arrange and braid it like the Saracens [Arabs].
>
> As to their clothing, one needs to know that men and women wear the same kind of garments and are therefore not easy to tell apart; and as these matters seem more curious than useful I have not troubled to write further about their clothing and adornment.

Both men and women wore tunics of buckram (cotton or linen), fine fabric, or silken fabric. They were cut open from the top downward and folded double across the breast, tied closed on the left side by a single cord and on the right by three. All fur clothes were made in like manner. Married women wore tunics that were cut open in front and hung down to the ground, along with a round headdress that stood up for a foot and a half, which they were never seen without in the presence of men.

From existing descriptions of Mongol men in Yesugei's day, most were short by today's standards, hardly ever exceeding five feet six. What they lacked in height they made up for in the broad expanse of their powerful chests. Their faces were flat, with black or brown piercing eyes set above high cheekbones, and mouths that revealed flashing white teeth when they smiled. Mongol women were noted for their beauty. Of all the distinguishing features of Mongols, none stood out more than their bowed legs, shaped to the flanks of their sturdy Mongolian ponies.

Because of the nomadic lifestyle of the Mongols, their cylindrical wicker-and-felt tents had to be portable, and a Mongol wife could dismantle a *ger* in less than an hour. Some were moved fully assembled. "The smallest are put on a cart drawn by one ox, the larger by two or three or more depending on how large it is and how many are needed to move," wrote John of Plano Carpini. "Whenever they travel, whether to war or other places, they always take their homes with them." Along with their homes, they also took all their belongings—clothing, beds, cupboards, chests, stoves, and family heirlooms.

All adult males shared the important responsibility of training boys and young-adult males—the future Mongol hunters and warriors—in horsemanship, the use of the bow and arrow, falconry, and other skills essential to their way of life. Mongols could fire their arrows with deadly accuracy while at a full gallop on their ponies.

These sturdy little beasts carried their riders unerringly through windstorms and blizzards, across furnace-like deserts under scorching suns, and up and down massive mountains for days on end. Young males learned to travel across uncharted expanses guided only by such navigational aids as the stars, the flight of wild geese and cranes, and their aptitude for recalling precisely the location of geographical landmarks over land once traveled.

When Mongol men engaged an enemy, their wives took over the duties normally performed by their husbands—making bows and arrows, saddles and saddle bags, and so on. Their own duties included driving the draft animals pulling carts, milking the cows and goats, cooking, making clothes, sewing the felt tents, and raising children. Clan and tribal leaders frequently sought and acted upon the advice of their wives.

The Mongols were a strongly spiritual people, believing devoutly in the existence of a soul that survives the body's death and in reincarnation. The Mongols believed there was one supreme power in the universe—Tengri (Eternal Heaven). But this belief differed from monotheism—belief in one god—in that they also believed in countless lesser spirits.

Spirits, they believed, dwelled everywhere—in lakes, forests, rivers, mountains, and in Earth itself. To help sort out an infinite number of spirits and demons, Mongols relied on the spiritual wizardry of shamans—tribal priests who claimed to own sole contact with the

A Mongol version of a demon spirit.

supreme and lesser deities. Mongols practiced their religious beliefs informally and privately. They attended no churches, said no prayers, and followed no established dogma or doctrine. Their belief in an infinite spirit world helped them to accept the faiths of others—Buddhism, Christianity, Islam, Taoism, and others—and later to allow their continued practice in conquered lands.

Mongols of high standing often selected their burial place ahead of time. Before the moment of death arrived, family and friends left the bedside of the dying person to allow him or her to embark on the final journey alone. An important person was buried with many valuables but without a burial mound to mark the grave. Such burials were frequently conducted at night and the gravesites trampled by many horses to prevent would-be grave robbers from looting them.

The already-tenuous life on the steppes became even more fragile for the Mongols when their tribes and clans began breaking up in the middle of the twelfth century. The kinship bonds that had previously held their patriarchal society together like the fish glue of their bows started breaking apart under pressures resulting from continual plundering and retaliatory campaigns. The thirteenth-century Mongol shaman Teg Tenegri described the times this way: "[T]he stars turned in the heavens. Everyone was feuding. Rather than sleep they robbed each other of their possessions. The earth and its crust had moved. The whole nation was in rebellion. Rather than rest they fought each other. In such a world one did not live as one wished, but rather in constant conflict. There was no respite, only battle. There was no affection, only mutual slaughter."

Loyalties had ceased to lay with tribes and kin. Instead, they were shifted to victorious warrior leaders who accumulated followings large and powerful enough to defeat and subjugate whole tribes or clans. In order to preserve their ill-gotten wealth and power, these emerging war lords were forced to perpetually engage in the recruitment and training of adventurous young men willing to become their followers (*nököd*) for a share of the loot and a chance to form their own following.

By the time Temujin was born, the Mongol people were scattered across the vast steppes. Divided by petty feuds and fights, they were weak and impoverished. But in the years to come, a powerful new leader would arise who would join them together into a mighty and destructive force.

2

Temujin

Much of the information available about Genghis Khan's life and rule was only recently discovered. For centuries, rumors had circulated that someone who knew the great khan well had written a history of him, but no evidence of any such account existed. When a text did surface in Beijing, China, in the 1800s, it was exceedingly difficult to translate. Not until the 1970s were chapters slowly, haltingly, brought into English. The first full American translation of *The Secret History of the Mongols* was published in 1982. Though accessing its treasures has not been easy, scholars have found *The Secret History* offers a wealth of incredibly detailed information about the Mongol leader and the times in which he lived.

Temujin spent his early childhood by the Onon River

The birth site of Temujin at the junction of the Onon River and the little Khorkh.

at the site of Yesugei's main camp. Hoelun, his mother, bore three more sons and a daughter in quick succession: Khasar, Khachun, Temuge-Otchigen, and Temulun, respectively. The names of three of their offspring derive from the common root of *temur* (iron). Otchigen means "prince of the hearth or fire." The title is added to the name of the youngest son in the family, who traditionally inherits the father's estate. Khasar, who was born within two years of Temujin, became Temujin's chief comrade as a boy and later served him well as a man.

Like all Mongol children, Temujin learned to ride at a young age and mastered the art of archery by targeting birds. In the winter, he and his brothers enjoyed playing on the iced-over Onon. Temujin's best friend was a boy named Jamuka. One winter, the two exchanged knucklebones cast in copper and declared themselves to be *andas*—sworn brothers (blood brothers). In the spring, they gave each other arrows with special tips and reaffirmed themselves as *andas*.

When Temujin was about ten, Yesugei began the process of finding a suitable wife for him. In keeping with the Mongol tradition of selecting a wife from a different tribe to create healthy bloodlines and build strong alliances, Yesugei looked to the Olkhunuud, Hoelun's tribe, for Temujin's future bride. The Olkhunuud lived on the eastern fringes of the Gobi, far to the south. Yesugei and Temujin set out on their long journey with only a small party, even though the route was difficult and treacherous. Upon the death of his father, Yesugei had inherited the leadership of a disparate group of Mongols from numerous clans. He had friends and relatives everywhere and did not fear for safe passage across the dangerous steppes.

Yesugei and his small party traveled east down the

Borte, the woman chosen to be Temujin's wife. *(Bibliothèque nationale de France, Paris)*

Kerulen River, then south. After threading their way between two mountains, they came upon a camp of Unggirad people, distant relatives of the Borijin, where they were greeted by Dei-sechen, the Unggirad chieftain, and given refreshments.

Dei-sechen was an accomplished man who had grown

wealthy trading with Chinese merchants. When he realized Yesugei was out to find a wife for his son, Dei-sechen saw a chance to advance his own interests. Dei-sechen just happened to have a young daughter about Temujin's age. He invited Yesugei into his tent to view his daughter, whose name was Borte. She was about a year older than Temujin. The two chieftains agreed on the future marriage of Temujin and Borte, for both men benefited in the arrangement. Yesugei acquired a promising daughter-in-law, and Dei-sechen gained an alliance with a powerful clan leader. Dei-sechen hosted a feast, and Yesugei gave his future in-law a fine horse as a betrothal gift.

Because it was the custom for a betrothed young man to remain with his future in-laws until the time of his marriage and subsequent return to his clan, Yesugei left Temujin behind and departed for home the next day.

On Yesugei's return trip, he encountered a band of Tatars who invited him to eat with them in the hospitable tradition of steppe travelers. Hoping they did not recognize him as a mortal enemy, and not wishing to offend them because of their superior numbers, he accepted their invitation. But the Tatars did recognize him and slipped poison into his food and drink. After resuming his journey, Yesugei fell deathly ill. Once home, he sent for a servant, Munlik, and asked him to bring Temujin home. Yesugei died before his messenger left camp.

Munlik carried out his task and quickly returned to the Mongol camp on the Onon with young Temujin.

Yesugei's death cast a pall over the fate of his followers. There was no other leader strong enough to hold the camp together. Temujin was still a boy and not yet capable of leading thousands of men. The disparate group soon began to break up, as the different clans went their separate ways. Hoelun and her family attached themselves to the Tayichiud tribe led by Targutai, who was one of the strongest chieftains. As the family of a former chieftain, they were treated well for a time, but when the Tayichiud moved off to summer pastures, Hoelun and her family were left behind as too many mouths to feed.

As Yesugei's former principal wife, Hoelun assumed the leadership role of the family. The little band now consisted of Hoelun and her five children; Yesugei's other wife, Sochigel, and her two sons; an old servant woman; and a few horses, sheep, and goats. Their chances for survival in that fierce land looked slim, but Hoelun was a woman of grit and determination: "Her cap firmly on her head and her dress girt around her knees, she ran up and down the Onon River collecting rowans [or pomes, the fleshy fruit of a Eurasian mountain ash] and bird cherries, feeding her chicks night and day." The boys hunted to help supply their daily fare, and so the little clan eked out a meager living for the next two years.

As Yesugei's sons grew, tension over male dominance in the clan began to build between Temujin and his older, bigger half brother Begter. One day, Temujin and Khasar caught a fish in the Onon, only to have Begter and his brother Belgutei snatch it from them. The offended brothers complained to Hoelun. "Recently they took from us a lark which we had shot with an arrow," they said. "Now they have robbed us again. How can we live with each other?" To preserve peace in the family, Hoelun advised her sons to save their anger for enemies outside the clan. In time, the day would come to avenge themselves against the Tayichiud who had cast them aside and left them to die. It was not the answer they wished to hear.

Temujin and Khasar stormed off, picked up their bows, and returned to the river where they found Begter tending the horses. They positioned themselves to the front and rear of him. Begter saw their bows and the fire in their eyes and realized he could not reason with them. Sitting down, he crossed his legs and folded his arms. At a signal from Temujin, the two boys raised their bows and shot Begter in the chest.

When Hoelun learned what they had done, she was furious. Even in the harsh environment of the steppes, men rarely murdered members of their own clans, particularly not their own relatives. Still, the elimination of Begter removed an ever-present source of problems within the family. From that point forward, Temujin's authority went unchallenged, and order took hold in the camp.

The little clan survived for two more years along the Onon River, employing all the survival skills passed down from their ancestors, while Temujin was growing shrewd and strong. Although the clan remained tucked away in a remote wooded valley between the Onon and the Kerulen Rivers, wayfarers occasionally passed through the region and carried news across the steppes of the survival of Yesugei's clan. Those who observed Hoelun and her brood focused much of their attention on Temujin, a lean and muscular youth of fourteen whose fierce, cat-like eyes, proud bearing, and finely chiseled face radiated authority. Tales of how he had slain his half brother echoed across the steppes. Eventually, these stories reached Targutai, the Tayichiud prince responsible for his clan's desertion of Hoelun and her family.

Targutai held a tribal council at which he announced that Hoelun's sons had come of age and now posed a threat to avenge themselves against those who had abandoned them. Of all the boys, Targutai feared only Temujin. The council decided to capture Temujin rather than to kill him, which might risk a tribal war with his relatives (though none had aided him in his time of need). Targutai led the raiding party.

When they reached Hoelun's campsite deep in the forest at the base of a cliff, the raiders shouted for Temujin to come out alone. Instead, Khasar, who had become an expert archer, unleashed a shower of arrows to discourage the Tayichiud, while Belgutei felled some saplings to form a barricade. That night Temujin, figuring the Tayichiud wanted him alone and would not harm the others, saddled a horse and tried to escape. The raiders spotted him and gave chase. Temujin fled into the woods and took shelter in a thicket. Targutai and his band encircled the thicket and waited for hunger and thirst to drive Temujin from his shelter.

After capturing Temujin, Targutai and his party returned to their *ordu* (camp or tent village) and restrained their prisoner in a *cangue* (a wooden collar, similar to an ox yoke, to which the hands of a prisoner were attached). Just how long Temujin remained an unwilling

This sixteenth-century painting depicts a prisoner restrained in a *cangue* much like the one used to hold Temujin. *(Museum of Inner Mongolia)*

guest of the Tayichiud is unclear, but on the Day of the Red Disk—the sixteenth day of the first full moon of summer on which Mongols feast and drink all day long—Temujin bashed his jailer in the head with his *cangue* and escaped after most of the revelers had retired for the night. He ran off along the Onon, found a small inlet, and submerged himself, *cangue* and all, with only his face above water. Meanwhile, his stunned keeper recovered and sounded the alarm.

Men bleary with drink and sleep stumbled out of their *gers* and began to comb the area for Temujin. One of the searchers, Sorgan Shira of the Suldus clan, saw Temujin in the water but did not alert the others. He had known and respected Yesugei the Brave. He told Temujin that the Tayichiud were jealous of him, but that he respected Temujin's courage. Sorgan Shira later told Temujin when it was safe to get out of the water and advised him to head for his mother's camp.

Temujin appreciated the man's help, but he had learned the art of survival. He knew he would not make it far across the rough country wearing a *cangue* and without a horse. He waited until later that night when sleep returned to the camp and made his way to the *ger* of Sorgan Shira. Although terrified to see Temujin, Sorgan Shira, fearing for the lives of his family and himself, nevertheless helped him a second time. He and his sons removed Temujin's *cangue* and burned it in their fire. They hid him in a cartload of wool for three days until the search for him subsided somewhat, at which time they gave him a mare, *airak* to drink, lamb's meat, and a bow and arrows, and sent him on his way.

Temujin never forgot the kindness of Sorgan Shira. Years later, he rewarded him with gifts of land, servants, and special privileges; and he made the sons of Sorgan Shira generals in his army. Among the many lessons Temujin learned in surviving his perilous youth was how to value true loyalty found outside the clan or tribe over the often empty claims of loyalty from blood relations.

After fleeing his captors, Temujin followed the Onon up into the hills for several days where he found his mother's new camp in the shadow of the great mountain called Burkhan Khaldun ("God Mountain"). Hoelun had fixed her camp on a stream by a small mountain lake.

Not long after Temujin rejoined his family, a band of raiders swept down on the camp and made off with eight of Hoelun's nine horses. The ninth horse—straw-yellow with a hairless tail—escaped theft only because Belgutei had gone off on it that morning to hunt marmots. When Belgutei returned, Temujin, over the objections of his brother, took the straw-yellow horse and went in pursuit of the thieves. Without horses, his family would perish.

Temujin followed their trail across the mountains and down the westward steppes. After riding for four days, he came upon a herd of horses belonging to a sturdily built young man about his own age. Temujin told him about the theft of his own horses and asked if he had seen them. The young man, whose name was Boorchu, told Temujin that tales of his escape from the Tayichiud had spread across the steppes. Many people, he said, admired Temujin for his courage and resourcefulness. Boorchu gave him a fresh mount and volunteered to help him recover his stolen horses.

The two young men rode off together across the steppes. On the third day, they came upon Temujin's horses in the midst of a larger herd outside the thieves'

Horses were an essential part of life on the steppes. *(Bibliothèque nationale de France, Paris)*

camp. No one seemed to be around so they cut Temujin's horses from the herd and drove them toward home. Eight men or more came bursting from their *gers* and chased after them for three days until finally giving up their pursuit. Safely back at the *ger* of his new friend, Temujin thanked Boorchu and offered him his pick of the rescued horses. Boorchu refused, explaining that he had ridden with Temujin only out of friendship.

The two young men then swore eternal friendship, a vow that was later affirmed by Boorchu's father. Boorchu's willingness to put his own life at risk to help a stranger in need demonstrated Temujin's innate ability to attract others to his cause. Boorchu became the first of many loyal followers to fall under the sway of the future conqueror.

When Temujin was about sixteen, he decided the time had come to claim Borte, his betrothed. With his half brother Belgutei, who had come to idolize him, Temujin headed south to claim his Unggirad bride-to-be. Dei-sechen, the wily Unggirad chieftain and father of the promised bride, was uncommonly delighted to see the Mongol youth whose fame was spreading. The wedding of Temujin and Borte took place at once, followed by the customary wedding feast. When the newlyweds left for Temujin's camp the next day, Dei-sechen sent along with Borte an exquisite black sable coat as a gift for Hoelun.

The sable coat was extremely valuable, but Temujin realized it could be even more valuable if he gave it away. He suggested to Hoelun that they use it to gain a powerful ally. Hoelun agreed to her son's plan. But first, Temujin sent Belgutei off across the mountains to ask Boorchu for his support. Boorchu saddled a horse and returned across the mountains with Belgutei. At a remote site on the Sanggur, Temujin and Boorchu swore the oath of brotherhood to become *andas*. Temujin then moved his clan to a new, more secure site—though still in the shadow of Burkhan Khaldun. Where before there had been three able-bodied men at the camp—Temujin, Khasar, and Belgutei—there were now four. Their numbers were small, but it was a start.

Temujin entered manhood with strong ambitions, relentless determination, and a sense that he was destined to become a great leader. Now that Borte was safely settled in his clan under the care and guidance of his mother, Temujin took his first step in realizing the destiny he foresaw for himself. He took the black sable cloak that Dei-sechen had intended as a wedding gift for Hoelun and rode off with his brothers Belgetei and Khasar to find Torghil, the powerful leader of the Kereyid tribe whose lands stretched across the Mongol homelands from the Onon River in the west to the Chinese frontier in the east. Much of the respect accorded to Torghil by the steppe peoples derived from his relationship with the Chinese emperor.

Many years before, Temujin's father and Torghil had sworn to be *andas*—blood brothers. In Torghil's camp at the headwaters of the Tuul River, Temujin stood before the khan of the Kereyids and said, "In earlier days you swore friendship with my father, [Yesugei]. Accordingly, you are as my own father and I bring you my wife's wedding gift." He then handed the coat to Torghil, who accepted the gift graciously.

"In gratitude for the black sable cloak I will reunite you with your people," he said. "In gratitude for the black sable cloak I will bring together again your dispersed people." In proclaming Torghil his adopted father, Temujin became his vassal. This meant that he placed himself in a subservient position and gave his loyalty to Torghil. In return, Torghil would protect Temujin and his family.

Torghil got something from the bargain, too: loyal friends and followers, which he needed because he worried about challenges to his throne from his own son, as well as from his uncle, the *gur-khan* (supreme khan or king).

Temujin's life entered a new phase. His relationship with Torghil, a respected—or at least feared—chieftain of a powerful tribe gave him new credibility. One example of his enhanced prestige came when an old man of the Oriangqadai tribe (distant relatives of the Mongols) came to Temujin's camp and presented his son, Jelme, to him as a squire or servant.

Although he was barely a man, Temujin's reputation for courage, resourcefulness, fairness, devotion to friends, and ferocity toward foes spread swiftly across the steppes. In the years to come, Temujin would attract thousands to his service. For the present, however, his following remained small—too small to help him cope with the greatest challenge of his young life. When word of Temujin's growing fame reached the Merkids in the west, their leading chieftain decided that the time had come to avenge Yesugei's abduction of Hoelun two decades before. They would do so by taking Temujin's wife, Borte.

3

A Heavenly Mandate

The Merkid chieftain called on his kinsmen for help, and the chieftains of the two other great divisions of the Merkid tribe answered his call. Three hundred strong, they waited until night to attack Temujin's camp. Sleeping on the ground in Hoelun's *ger*, the old servant woman, Khoakchin, felt the vibration of their hoofbeats while they were still some distance away. She rose and awakened Hoelun.

Hoelun woke the children quickly. Temujin and his brothers ran for their horses. With a clan of twelve people and nine horses, only nine could flee. Temujin helped Hoelun and his sister Temulun to mount, then leaped on a third horse. His four brothers and his two followers, Boorchu and Jelme, scrambled aboard the remaining six horses and took flight. Borte, Temujin's

Temujin's wife, Borte, was kidnapped by the Merkids and taken back to her original homeland. *(Bibliothèque nationale de France, Paris)*

stepmother Sochigel, and old Khoakchin were left behind and captured by the vengeful Merkids.

The idea of six warriors running away and leaving three helpless women to face imminent danger alone might seem less than chivalrous, but Temujin and the others who had fled exercised the only reasonable option open to them. Temujin knew that the Merkids wanted to kidnap Borte—not kill her—and that they likely would take the other women into their clans as servants. On the other hand, if those who fled had remained to defend Borte and the other women against such overwhelming odds, they most certainly would have been killed. By fleeing, Temujin had saved most of his clan, and had remained alive and able to confront the Merkids under more favorable circumstances.

Borte, Sochigel, and Khoakchin were captured easily. The Merkids roamed about for a time looking for Temujin before returning to their homelands. The fugitives escaped to a dense forest at the foot of Burkhan Khaldun, where they hid for three days. Boorchu and Jelme tracked the Merkids to make sure they had left the region.

Temujin spent the next three days in deep prayer, giving thanks to Burkhan Khaldun ("God Mountain") and to the Eternal Blue Sky for the deliverance of himself and his family. "The Burkhan has preserved my life like that of a louse and I have conquered great fear," he said. "I will honor the *Burkhan-Khaldun* with sacrifices every morning and pray to it every day. My children and my children's children shall be mindful of this." After praying to the mountain, he turned toward the sun, knelt nine times, and offered a libation of mare's milk and a prayer to the sun. Temujin also prayed for guidance in deciding what to do about Borte's kidnapping.

Borte's abduction left him with three choices: He

The Burkhan Khaldun where Temujin went to pray after the Merkid's attack.

could follow the Kerulen River downstream to the steppes and become a herder, possibly losing his herds to marauding tribes. He could return to the Onon, the place of his birth, where it was more secluded but lacked pastures for animals and would mean living off fish, birds, rats, and other small mammals. Or he could follow the Tuul River southwest to the domain of Torghil, khan of the Kereyid, and ask for his help.

The first two options would mean giving up on Borte and possibly finding another wife elsewhere. No one would expect him to attempt her rescue with only his tiny group to challenge the powerful Merkids. Finding another wife would not be easy, though, for few families would betroth a daughter to a man who had already lost a wife to more powerful men.

Temujin despaired over the loss of his beloved Borte. He decided to fight to get her back. This decision marked the defining moment of his life.

Temujin, with Khasar and Belgutei, traveled to Torghil's *ordu* (court or camp) to seek his adopted father's help. Torghil had not forgotten Temujin's gift of a black sable cloak. Beyond any sense of gratitude he might have felt for the gift, he also had nurtured a long-standing feud with the Merkids. Temujin's request for assistance in reclaiming Borte gave him an excuse to attack and loot them again. Torghil told Temujin to ask Jamuka for help.

Jamuka was chief of the Jadaran tribe—and the same Jamuka who had twice sworn the oath of brotherhood with Temujin when both men were youths playing on the iced-over Onon. Jamuka was also descended from a brother of Khabul Khan, and as such was Temujin's third cousin. Temujin sent his brothers to Jamuka's camp with Torghil's words and a personal message, reminding Jamuka of their sworn brotherhood. The Jadaran leader replied at once, promising vengeance.

Torghil and Jamuka assembled their armies near Burkhan Khaldun, along with a lesser *tumen* (regiment) of volunteers gathered by Temujin. These herdsmen on horseback resembled the Mongol armies of future fame only in that they were armed and mounted.

Their shortcomings aside, these ragtag *tumens*—with Torghil on the right, Jamuka on the left, and Temujin somewhere in between—crossed the mountains and descended into Merkid country. Their combined forces routed the Merkids, and for the most part, their raid was crowned with success. Temujin sent word to Torghil: "I

This map shows the homelands of the Mongols in relation to their neighbors.

have found my necessity which I sought."

Temujin had recovered Borte and exacted his revenge. Both Temujin and his *anda* Jamuka had distinguished themselves in the savage fighting. All three hundred of the Merkids who had attacked Temujin's clan and carried off Borte were slaughtered. The avengers failed to find Temujin's stepmother, Sochigel, and the old servant woman, Khoakchin, but they otherwise accomplished their mission. Temujin thanked Torghil and Jamuka for their help. Torghil returned to his camp; Temujin—now with a large following of his own—accompanied Jamuka back to his camp. Most of Temujin's new followers joined him there. The blood brothers had been reunited.

Soon after Borte's return, the news that she was pregnant marred her reunion with Temujin. While captive, she had been given as a wife to the brother of

Hoelun's first (and now deceased) husband. The birth of Borte's first son was cause for celebration, but the boy's paternity remained in doubt in Temujin's mind. Temujin named the boy Jochi, which means "visitor" or "guest" (or possibly "the unexpected"). Despite Jochi's uncertain parentage, Temujin never treated him any differently from his other sons, but the stigma of possible illegitimacy haunted Jochi throughout his life.

After being reunited in their campaign against the Merkids, Temujin and Jamuka declared themselves *andas* for a third time and exchanged gifts of valuables they had looted from the Merkids. Temujin gave Jamuka a golden belt and one of his best horses, a bay mare with a black mane and tail. Jamuka reciprocated in like fashion, presenting his *anda* with a similar gold belt and a fine gray horse. They then feasted, drank, and celebrated in the vigorous Mongol tradition. Having shared the experience of battle, they had now affirmed their brotherhood with both words and deeds.

These two young warriors had much in common. Like Temujin, Jamuka had known difficulties early in life: "As a small child I was deserted by my father and mother. I have no brothers. My wife is a shrew. I have untrustworthy companions." And like Temujin, Jamuka was highly ambitious, perceptive, courageous, adventuresome, and a natural leader. Destiny or chance appears to have brought this dynamic pair together at the right time for both. Jamuka needed a companion he could trust, and Temujin needed a strong ally to lend him protection while he gathered a powerful following of his own.

After consulting with Hoelun, Temujin decided to join forces with Jamuka. Despite Jamuka's superior numbers, Temujin entered into the union feeling himself the equal of Jamuka. But Jamuka considered Temujin his follower. This mutual misconception did not interfere with their harmonious relationship, however. The two men were inseparable. They did everything together—even slept away from the others under the same blanket.

In the steppe culture, smell plays an important role in expressing deep feelings. Rather than hugging or kissing to say hello or good-bye, steppe nomads sniff one another in a gesture similar to a kiss on the cheek. Like a hug or a kiss, a sniff can convey various emotions: love, friendship, sadness, etc. Temujin's people believed a person's odor housed a part of their soul. For Jamuka and Temujin to share a blanket in their own *ger* showed the depth of their connection and their trust in each other.

The camps and herds of Jamuka and Temujin moved together from pasture to pasture. Winter came. Snow blanketed the steppes, and the nomads huddled in their *gers*. Food became scarce, and the animals suffered from hunger. When spring finally arrived, the two camps moved on to find lush, green pastures. Their animals grew fat, and their people ate well. When the August sun scorched the earth, animals and people made do with less. Winter swept in again from the north. The people

When they weren't away at war, Mongol men were expected to hunt and work in the *ger* camps. *(Bibliothèque nationale de France, Paris)*

huddled through another long winter, sustained by stored meats and ample supplies of fermented mare's milk. Over time, Borte gave Temujin two more sons: Chagatai and Ogodei. Sons were considered good omens and good luck, and were welcomed into the tribe.

Many of the neighboring Mongol leaders were observing Temujin's courage, leadership skills, and how he rewarded and advanced his followers in accordance with their abilities and how well they performed. Boorchu, the son of a minor chieftain, and Jelme, the son of a wandering blacksmith, were becoming great men under Temujin. After the Merkid raid, Temujin's generosity in sharing among his followers the captured serfs and flocks did not go unnoticed. The leaders of some of the tribes subservient to the Tayichiud said to each other, "The Prince [Temujin] dresses his people in his own clothes, he permits them to ride his own horses; this man could certainly bring peace to the tribe and rule the nation."

But these leaders did not want to commit to following Temujin so long as he was allied with Jamuka. The complicated politics of the steppe meant Jamuka could technically claim to be Temujin's superior because he was descended from the more significant branch of their common ancestors. Though Temujin comported himself as if he and Jamuka were coleaders, the time was nearing when Jamuka would exert his authority in an effort to dominate his best friend.

The day began like so many others during the past year and a half, with Jamuka and Temujin riding at the head of the long column of their followers and animals, moving toward new grazing lands. At midday, Jamuka pulled up suddenly and announced he wanted to make camp.

It made no sense to stop their migration after only half a day's journey, but Temujin said nothing. Instead, he dropped back and waited for Hoelun and Borte to move up in the train in order to seek their advice. Both women agreed Temujin should ignore Jamuka's order and ride on.

Jamuka might have been trying to exert his authority

over Temujin by giving his followers a more desirable campsite by the mountain and relegating Temujin and his people to a less attractive site by the river. He might also have felt that Temujin was becoming too popular and was intentionally provoking him. He might have just been tired, or he might have acted on any of a hundred other impulses. Whatever the reason, when Jamuka and his clan stopped to camp, Temujin and his followers kept going. The time had come to choose sides. Many of Jamuka's people broke off to join Temujin; many more remained. The two blood brothers parted that day without violence, but for the next twenty-five years, they would wage a constant battle for supremacy over the steppes.

In time, both Temujin and Jamuka expanded their followings, but loyalties shifted back and forth, and neither chief managed to fuse their brethren into a solid nation comparable in strength to the more powerful Kereyid, Tatar, and Naiman tribes.

Rumors began to circulate across the steppes that Temujin possessed a heavenly mandate and was destined to become lord of the realm. Khorchi, the principal chieftain of the Baarin tribe, told Temujin of a vision in which he had seen a hornless white ox uproot the great pole of Jamuka's tent and drag it to Temujin's camp. In Khorchi's dream, the bull bellowed: "Heaven and Earth have agreed that [Temujin] shall be Lord of the Empire. I bring him this Empire."

Khorchi, who was aligned with Jamuka, then asked

Temujin what kind of reward he might expect for defecting and bringing news of this vision confirming Temujin's heavenly mandate. Temujin had to promise great riches and many wives to the Baarin leader, but he hoped Khorchi's support would pay off.

Temujin's gamble worked. Among the superstitious Mongols, tales such as the one Khorchi told carried great persuasive powers. Over the ensuing days, weeks, months, and years, followers flocked from many clans to join Temujin. By the summer of 1189, he felt strong enough to challenge Jamuka for the rule of all Mongols.

Temujin summoned his followers to a *khuriltai* on the steppe, at the base of the Heart-Shaped Mountain. His intent was to become khan of all he surveyed. The number of influential leaders that attended would determine Temujin's fate. In the end, not all the tribes in the region sent representatives, but enough came that the group could make the ceremonial declaration. Temujin was officially made a khan. His followers pledged to bring him women and fine horses and vowed their loyalty in battle and in peace.

Temujin could not be called khan of all the Mongols because Jamuka still ruled over more than half those people. Neither was he named Genghis Khan on this occasion. That name implies "ruler of the world." Many battles remained to be fought before Temujin could legitimately claim the name of Genghis Khan.

Claiming the 7itle

Temujin's first official acts as khan were to establish a basic administrative system and a formal organization of services to facilitate his rule and to ensure the efficient operation of all functions essential to tribal life. He conducted his affairs out of a chief's complex of *gers* that served as his tribal center. This complex was known as an *ordu* or *horde* (which later gave rise to the phrase "Mongol hordes"). In assigning responsibility for various services and duties, he continued his policy of rewarding faithful followers, regardless of kinship. He arranged his followers into groups of Quiver Bearers and Sword Bearers, making some responsible for food supplies, others for beverages, and still others for the horses, sheep, and other animals.

For security, he formed an elite bodyguard of 150

warriors—seventy day guards and eighty night guards. These guards surrounded the camp at all times. After assigning responsibilities necessary to a smooth-running camp, Temujin Khan rewarded his most faithful followers, Boorchu and Jelme. These two would always rank over all others as his strong right and left arms.

Next, Temujin sent two messengers to Torghil and another two to Jamuka with news of his election as khan. Torghil, naively believing that Temujin would always be his loyal subject, responded encouragingly to Temujin's messengers. Jamuka was similarly polite, but sent an angry message to two of Temujin Khan's new followers asking why they supported Temujin over him. Jamuka would soon make his true feelings toward his sworn brother known—not in words but in deeds.

In the meantime, Temujin set to work organizing and training an effective army. He began with a small nucleus of men who had shown themselves to be totally loyal to him. These men had no followers of their own and thus stood to gain or lose everything under his leadership. Temujin made these men captains and gave them groups of horsemen to command. Most of these men were young and enthusiastic, men like Boorchu's kinsman Ogolai and Jelme's brother Subodei, who would one day become the greatest Mongol general of all.

The new khan quickly put together an army like none ever seen before among the Mongols. Under his guidance, each captain drilled his body of horsemen in mock battles. Again and again, the riders executed unique

This Persian painting by Rashid al-Din shows Mongol warriors training for combat. They practiced using their bows on horseback without arrows in order to perfect the famed "Parthian Shot" in which neither horse nor rider breaks stride when the arrow is released. *(Bibliothèque nationale de France, Paris)*

mounted maneuvers on command until every rider in every group reacted as one to every command. The Mongols were trained to charge forward in attack, then wheel about and feign retreat to draw the enemy closer. They could fire their arrows with deadly accuracy, then turn to attack again a decimated enemy. Mongols avoided close hand-to-hand combat for fear of coming into contact with another man's blood. Believing scent and blood to be the repository of a man's soul, Mongols avoiding touching blood they had spilled or even being close enough to smell their enemies.

While the warriors of other steppe tribes fought savagely, they lacked the discipline and unity of action that can only be acquired through constant practice. On occasion, other armies still could and did defeat Temujin's forces. When defeated, however, Temujin's troops would withdraw in an orderly way with their leaders, regroup, and prepare to fight again. In 1191, about a year after Temujin became khan, his developing army met its first test.

One afternoon, Taichar, Jamuka's younger brother, confiscated a herd of horses grazing on his land. The horses belonged to Jochi Darmala, one of Temujin's followers. That night, Jochi circled Taichar's camp, let loose a shower of arrows, rounded up his horses, and drove them off. One of his arrows struck Taichar in the spine and killed him instantly. News of his brother's death at the hands of one of Temujin's men infuriated Jamuka. He quickly raised an army of some 30,000 men and launched an unexpected attack on Temujin. At this point, Temujin's training program had not matured and did not lend much advantage to Temujin. Jamuka defeated him handily, killing or capturing many of his forces and driving off the rest in confusion.

Despite his convincing victory over Temujin, Jamuka

Jamuka's prisoners were boiled alive in cauldrons, a practice that served to
spread the Mongol's reputation of savagery and terror among the steppe peoples.
(Bibliothèque nationale de France, Paris)

remained angry upon his return to camp. He ordered
seventy of the male captives to be boiled alive in cauldrons. According to Mongol belief, this kind of death
destroys not only the victim's physical being but his soul
as well: the victim is eliminated from this world and the
next. Jamuka then severed the head of another of his
captives, tied it to his horse's tail, and dragged it about
behind him, thereby defiling the man's soul and casting
shame upon his family.

In the end, Jamuka's savagery worked against him
and for Temujin. Because of Jamuka's needless atroci-
ties, two large clans—the Uru'uts and the Mangquts—
defected from his following and joined with Temujin.
Among those who left Jamuka and joined Temujin were

Munlik, Yesugei's old servant, and his seven sons. One of these was Kokochu, an important shaman later known as Teb Tengeri. Those who remained in Jamuka's camp had reason to worry, for under the rule of an irrational, ruthless leader, the fate of the boiled and headless victims might someday become their own. Now that Jamuka had revealed his true face, the struggle for mastery over all the Mongols could begin in earnest.

After Temujin's first defeat as khan, the record of his life disappears for some five or six years. The next thing known is that around 1196, Temujin learned that a faction within the Kereyids had deposed his adopted father Torghil and cast him out to wander aimlessly and vulnerable in the Gobi. He finally took refuge with a khan in Turkistan. Temujin acted swiftly to raise a large army and attack Torghil's enemies. Once Torghil's khanate was restored, Temujin joined his patron in an attack against the Merkids. They subdued and plundered the Merkids in short order. Temujin's standing as a powerful steppe leader grew for his part in the two fights, but greater political forces were at work over the eastern horizon.

The Jurched (Chin Empire) rulers of Cathay (China) routinely played one steppe tribe against another to prevent any given tribe from becoming too powerful and thus a threat to their empire. Recently, they had become annoyed at the growing insolence of the Tatars and their refusal to pay tribute. They decided to enlist the aid of Torghil to remove the Tatar nuisance. Torghil again called on Temujin for help. Eager to take revenge on the Tatars, Temujin quickly called an army together.

In the winter of 1196, Temujin made ready to attack the Tatars. He waited six days for the arrival of the Jurkins, a tribe of Mongol lineage that lived to the south along the Kerulen River. They had pledged to take part in the upcoming campaign but failed to show up. Temujin left without them to join Torghil. Together, Temujin and Torghil readily defeated the Tatars. Their easy victory shifted the balance of power on the steppes. The Chin, delighted, awarded Torghil the title of Ong (or Wang) Khan and bestowed the lesser title of *Ja'utquri* ("keeper of the frontier") upon Temujin.

Temujin returned from the Tatar campaign to find that the Jurkins, who should have joined him in battle, had instead waited for him to leave and then raided his base camp. He quickly made his neighbors to the south the focus of his next military adventure and subdued them with ease in 1197. Temujin now introduced a second radical change in traditional ruling styles: instead of looting his defeated enemies and leaving them to their own devices to survive, he assimilated them into his own tribe—and not just as servants or serfs but as members with full tribal privileges. Moreover, he set an example for others to follow by adopting an orphaned Jurkin boy into his own family, to be raised as his own brother. In this way, Temujin's followers multiplied at a phenomenal rate, and with each conquest he became stronger and stronger.

EMPIRE IN THE EAST

BURI THE WRESTLER

In the winter of 1196, Temujin hosted a feast. He invited the Jurkins to attend, hoping to enlist their aid in his coming campaign against the Tatars. During the festivities, an incident developed between Belgutei, who was assigned to guard the horses, and Buri Boko, his Jurkin counterpart. When one of the guests who had sipped a little too much mare's milk attempted to steal a bridle from one of Temujin's horses, he was caught and brought before Belgutei. Buri Boko, who was known as Buri the Wrestler, went to Belgutei and demanded the thief's release.

Belgutei grabbed Buri's clothing and pulled him away from the prisoner. Buri, who was an undefeated wrestler, elected not to fight Belgutei hand to hand but rather drew his sword and sliced Belgutei's shoulder so that the blood ran down his arm. In the Mongol world, drawing another's blood that way constituted a grave insult. Belgutei, being a man of extreme good nature, let the insult pass and released the prisoner rather than disrupt the festive occasion. Temujin was less affable. The insult would cost Buri the Wrestler his life.

A year later, after Temujin had subjugated the Jurkins and assimilated them into his tribe, he summoned Buri the Wrestler and Belgutei for a wrestling match. Buri allowed himself to be thrown rather than provoke his new leader. Belgutei then seized Buri's shoulders and mounted him like a pony. On a signal from Temujin, Belgutei plunged his knee into Buri's spine and snapped it like a piece of kindling. Belgutei then dragged his paralyzed opponent outside the camp and left him to die alone.

After defeating the Jurkins, Temujin shifted his growing numbers downstream on the Kerulen River and established a new base camp on an island. The Mongols called it Khodoe Aral, which means "Barren Island."

The island stands amid a large, open, and treeless prairie, about 130 miles below Burkhan Khaldun and Temujin's birthplace on the Onon River. Renamed Avarga, this camp later became the first Mongol capital and the center of the Mongol universe. From 1197 to the end of Temujin's life, it remained his base of operations.

Over the next four years, Temujin and his followers prospered. Despite his growing strength, Temujin remained in a subservient role to Ong Khan (Torghil), and together they campaigned across the steppes. Yet even in the face of Temujin's increasing dominance, Jamuka stubbornly refused to recognize his leadership.

In 1201, Jamuka decided to challenge his *anda's* authority over the Mongols. He gathered a group of malcontents for a *khuriltai*. Among those who came were the Merkids, the Naimans, the Tayichiuds, the remnants of the Tatars, and even Borte's relatives, the Unggirads. The assembled tribes elected Jamuka as their leader, naming him Gur-khan (khan of all khans) and pledging to take to the field against Temujin. A series of steppe wars had begun.

In the winter of 1201–1202, Jamuka confronted the numerically superior forces of Ong Khan and Temujin near the Khalkha River. Each side brought shamans who chanted and beat drums to try to intimidate the other side. As the battle began, a terrible storm swept down on Jamuka's forces. "We have not been loved by Heaven," they cried, and scattered in all directions. Temujin chased after the fleeing Tayichiuds and Ong Khan pursued

Jamuka, who eventually took refuge with the Naimans.

Because Jamuka's forces fled the battlefield, his reign as supreme khan had ended almost before it began, but the final showdown between him and Temujin was still to come.

Temujin caught up with the Tayichiud along the Onon River. The fighting was fierce. Temujin took an arrow in the neck at nightfall and fell unconscious. Jelme came to his aid. Fearing the arrow had been poisoned, he sucked the blood from Temujin's wound for most of the night. To keep from offending the Earth or defiling his leader's soul, Jelme refrained from spitting the blood on the ground until he became too full to swallow any more. Finally, he spat and a small pool of blood collected nearby. When Temujin regained consciousness in the morning, he saw the pooled blood and said to Jelme, "Couldn't you have spit it somewhere else?"

The Tayichiud did not know that Temujin was injured. Under the cover of darkness, they dispersed and the fight was over. Temujin never forgot how Jelme saved him.

The climax of the steppe wars came in 1202 when Ong Khan sent Temujin on another punitive expedition against the Tatars. To maintain discipline, Temujin instituted a radical change in the way the campaign was conducted. Prior to engaging the Tatars again, he told his troops: "When we rout the enemy we will not halt to take booty. When the victory is decided the booty belongs to us collectively and I will distribute it. If we are repulsed

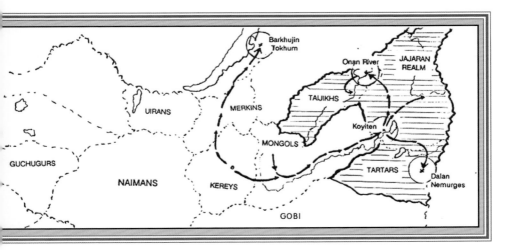

In 1201, Temujin and Torghil routed Jamuka's league at Koyiten. Later in the year, Temujin crushed the Tayichiuds along the banks of the Onon. In spring of 1202, the Mongols again defeated the Tayichiuds at Dalan Nemurges.

by the enemy we will reform on the spot from which we launched our attack. Any man who does not reform on the spot from which we attacked will be executed."

Temujin also decreed that a slain soldier's share of any acquired plunder would be given to each widow and to each orphan. This provision strengthened his soldier's loyalty and earned Temujin the further adoration of the poor. He showed a concern for his people that only increased their already fervent support for him.

In the final battle of the steppe wars, Temujin virtually massacred the Tatar soldiers along the Khalkha River. His men rounded up the survivors, which turned out to be thousands of people—some men and hundreds of women and children. The problem became what to do with them.

Temujin called an impromptu *khuriltai*. There it was

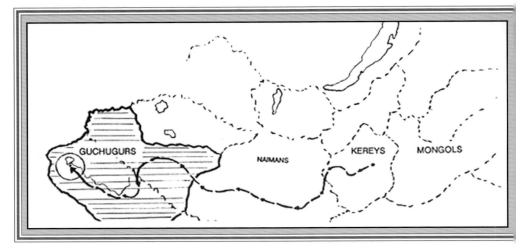

In August 1202, Temujin and his allies marched westward into Guchugurs country and wiped out the Guchugurs leader, King Buyirugh.

decided that the Mongols would execute all Tatar males taller than the linchpin holding the wheels on a cart— a designation which effectively eliminated all those on the verge of adulthood. The rest of the people would be assimilated into the Mongol tribe. To set an example, Temujin adopted another Tatar child into his family and took two Tatar wives: Yesugen and her elder sister Yesui. The Mongols took in so many Tatars that over time the names Tatar and Mongol became all but synonymous. It is a mark of Temujin's unique and charismatic leadership style that his people were willing and able to welcome their former enemies into the fold.

After the defeat of the Tatars, Ong Khan and Temujin controlled all of the eastern steppes. Temujin now felt that the time had come to cement his alliance with Ong Khan and proposed a marriage between his eldest son, Jochi, and Ong Khan's daughter. Ong Khan at first agreed to the proposal, but his son Senggum, who was a capable general in his own right and fiercely jealous of Temujin, opposed the idea. He talked his father into rejecting Temujin's proposal, and the relationship between Temujin and Ong Khan began to deteriorate. In future battles on the steppes, they would not fight as well together. On several occasions, Temujin narrowly averted defeat when expected relief by Ong Khan's forces failed to appear. Ong Khan and Senggum began to plot to eliminate Temujin and his threat to their superiority on the steppes. After trying and failing twice to lure Temujin into assassination attempts, they decided to assault him with an overwhelmingly superior force. Senggum appointed Jamuka to lead their army.

Two Tseren horseherds in the Kereyid camp overheard the plans and warned Temujin about the projected attack. In the ensuing battle of Khalakhaljit, Temujin's complete defeat was averted only when Senggum was badly injured. During the battle, Temujin's third son, Ogodei, was also seriously wounded, but both men would recover. Temujin and almost 5,000 of his followers fled eastward and regrouped on the shores of muddy Lake Baljuna.

The Baljuna period of 1203 was a crucial test for Temujin and his followers. They survived by eating horsemeat and drinking muddy water. Temujin swore this oath to his people: "When I have completed this great task I will share the bitter and sweet fruits with you. If I break my word, may I become as the waters of Baljuna." In return, Temujin's followers swore eternal allegiance to him, which became known as the Baljuna Covenant, and they toasted one another with the muddy waters of Baljuna.

Those who shared the experience at the muddy lake would forever hold a special standing with their revered leader. They became known as *Baljuntu*, or "Muddy Water Drinkers."

As often happened when Temujin found himself in dire straits, a number of tribes soon rallied around him and he quickly rebuilt a sizeable army. At the same time, after the fighting at Khalakhaljit, Ong Khan's forces—now under the leadership of his son Senggum—were showing signs of dissent. Temujin decided to resort to some trickery of his own. When he felt strong enough, Temujin launched a surprise attack on the Kereyids at Mount Jeje'er, in the western part of Mongol country. He caught them totally off guard.

Probably the most important battle of the Mongol leader's career, the battle of Mount Jeje'er pitted Temujin and his followers against a numerically superior foe. Defeat was no option for Temujin. After the beating he took at Khalakhaljit, another defeat at Jeje'er would likely have ended his ability to ever lead his fellow Mongols again.

Temujin and his followers swept down onto the steppes to encircle the Kereyids in a devastating surprise attack. The Mongol warriors fought like never before, and, finally, after three days of savage bloodletting, Temujin emerged victorious.

The aging Ong Khan and his son Senggum fled the

Mongol fighters were known for their intimidating approach to battle, complete with war cries and tricks on horseback to boast their skill and prowess.

battlefield into the desert where they were separately captured by hostile tribes and slain. Continuing his policy of integrating defeated enemies into his tribe, Temujin not only assimilated the Kereyids into his expanding Mongol nation, but praised them and ordered that they not be punished. To encourage their acceptance, he took several Kereyid princesses into his family and gave them as wives to his sons.

After the defeat of the Kereyids, only the powerful Naiman tribe stood between Temujin and his total domination of the eastern steppes (Mongol Plateau). When Jamuka's forces had deserted him during the thunderstorm in the winter of 1201-1202, he had sought refuge with the Naimans, who lived between the Selenga River and the Altai Mountains. There, he plotted his revenge.

Temujin called a *khuriltai* to plan the campaign against the Naimans. Victory would end all tribal conflicts on the plateau; defeat would send him to oblivion.

The Mongols prepared for battle as never before. Temujin restructured his army in groups of tens, hundreds, and thousands, and reorganized his command structure for more efficient control of these newly formed groups. Warned by spies in the enemy camp that the Naiman leader Tayang Khan was already advancing against him, Temujin set his new war machine in motion. In 1204, he moved across the steppes to meet the Naiman khan.

The two armies collided at the base of a mountain. Temujin surveyed the situation. Tayang had a considerably larger army composed of the Naimans, some Merkids, a few Tatars, and Jamuka and his Mongols. They were positioned with their backs to the mountain. When Temujin felt his men were ready, his army of some 80,000 men attacked with a savage fury rarely seen on the steppes and drove Tayang's forces, including Tayang Khan, his advisors, and Jamuka, far up the mountainside.

From the ferocity of their fighting, Temujin's four top generals would come to be known as the Four Hounds of Genghis Khan. Jebe (the Tayichiud), Khubilai (of the Barulas), Jelme (the son of a wandering Urianqqadai smith), and Subodei (Jelme's brother) won infamy for their prowess in battle, giving rise to countless legends

Opposite: Jebe, one of the "Four Hounds," illustrated here riding into battle in front of Temujin, was known for his accuracy and speed when shooting arrows.

and myths.

Observing the battle unfolding below, Jamuka could see his men stood little chance against Temujin's new formations. He and his army slipped away into the hills. Soon afterward, Tayang Khan was gravely wounded while attempting to flee the battleground. Without the support of Jamuka's Mongols, many of the Merkids fled. And without their leader Tayang, the Naimans lost heart and were soundly thrashed by Temujin's army. The Naiman khan died of his wound just after the fighting ceased, and his son Guchlug, who stood to inherit his father's rule, fled to the west.

In the battle's aftermath, Temujin's men brought before him a captive by the name of Tatatonga. An educated man, he introduced himself as Tayang Khan's seal bearer. On finding him literate, Temujin—who could not read or write himself but recognized the value of the written word—immediately took him into the tribe and assigned him the task of teaching all of his children and those of his principal nobles the meaning of scripted symbols and how to use them to communicate.

In the autumn of 1204, Temujin mounted one last campaign against the troublesome Merkids and quickly killed or captured most of them and assimilated the rest. He took another wife for himself, Hulan, who later became his favorite and accompanied him on many expeditions of conquest. His strength and fame continued to grow.

Jamuka and Temujin were reunited in an unexpected

way the next year. Hoping to win the new khan's favor, some of Jamuka's followers kidnapped him and brought him before Temujin. But they underestimated the premium Temujin placed on loyalty and trustworthiness. He ordered Jamuka's captors executed in front of their betrayed leader. Now that Jamuka could no longer hurt him, Temujin cared little for revenge. "Let us be companions," he implored his *anda* and arch nemesis. "Now, we are joined together once again, we should remind each other of things we have forgotten."

Jamuka responded angrily, "[W]hat use is there in my becoming a companion to you? On the contrary, sworn brother, in the black night I would haunt your dreams, in the bright day I would trouble your heart."

Rather than attempt reconciliation, Jamuka asked to be put to death in a way suiting his status: without spilling his blood on the earth or exposing it to the sun or the sky. "Kill me and lay down my dead bones in the high ground," he asked. "Then eternally and forever, I will protect the seed of your seed, and become a blessing for them." Temujin granted his sworn brother's request. Jamuka was wrapped in a blanket and crushed to death. His blood neither touched the earth nor saw the sun or sky, and thus his soul—which the Mongols believed resided in the blood—passed over to the other side. His crushed body was then buried in a high place with great ceremony where his spirit could watch over the steppes for the rest of time.

With the defeat of the Naimans and the death of his

archrival Jamuka, Temujin now ruled supreme over all the Mongols and all the other nomad tribes on the Mongolian Plateau. Still, he wanted confirmation of his status as ruler of what he called the "People of the Felt Walls." This clever phrase encompassed all Turco-Mongol people of the steppes and emphasized their common way of living over their tribal differences. Temujin returned to his sacred site in the shadow of "God Mountain" on the Onon River and called for a *khuriltai*.

In 1206, the people of the steppes gathered along the Onon by the hundreds of thousands, their presence signaling their vote to acclaim the greatest khan of all. Temujin's followers placed him on a black felt carpet and named him Genghis Khan—ruler of the world. At the age of forty-four, Temujin had claimed the highest title in the land.

Right and Might

The *khuriltai* of 1206 was a grand and festive affair with hundreds of thousands of steppe peoples gathered along the Onon River in the heart of Mongol country. Lines of *gers* stretched for miles in every direction. For days on end, there was singing, dancing, drinking, the throbbing of drums, and the playing of traditional Mongol games known as *naadam*—horse racing, archery, and wrestling. At the center of it all stood Temujin's *sulde*, a white standard with nine yak tails representing the nine Mongol tribes. Teb Tengeri, a shaman, set the tone for the crowning of the greatest Mongol chieftain ever: "God spoke to me, saying: 'I have given the whole Earth to [Temujin] and his sons and I have named him Genghis Khan. See that he rules justly.'" Genghis Khan now held sway over more than a million people in a land the size

A grassy plain along the Onon River where Temujin was most likely crowned Genghis Khan.

of today's Europe. He named this new sovereignty *Yeke Mongol Ulus*—the Great Mongol Nation.

Now forty-four, Genghis Khan had emerged from a nightmarish world of constant conflict and shifting alliances. He fully realized that his status and security hinged on the stability of his following, so he took immediate steps to solidify his power base. One of his first moves was to award his adopted son Mukali, one of the great generals known as the Four Coursers, the title of Go-ong, or Imperial Prince. He then sent Jebe, one of the Four Hounds, in pursuit of Guchlug, son of the Naiman king Tayang Khan. Rewarding loyalty and performance over kinship as usual, he reorganized his army into units of one thousand, and made each unit's leader one of his more prized followers. Because his army numbered roughly 95,000 men at the time, he named ninety-five new leaders.

The coronation of Genghis Khan is portrayed in this painting by Rashid al-Din as an event involving much pomp and ceremony. Although the specific customs and clothing depicted in the scene are more Chinese and Persian than Mongol, the grandness of the event is thought to be authentic. Genghis is attended by many courtiers as well as his two eldest sons, Jochi and Ogodei, who stand to his right. The white yak-tail standards to his left represent Mongol glory and authority. *(Bibliothèque nationale de France, Paris)*

Faced with a civil populace of more than a million people and an army of almost 100,000, Genghis Khan needed to reorganize and revitalize his methods of controlling civil and military affairs.

Traditionally, whenever a new empire was established on the steppes, the new khan would establish rules or laws by which he would govern. Genghis Khan's rules of governance are known as the *Yasa*, which means "order" or "decree." The *Yasa* was thought to have been conceived by Genghis Khan during the *khuriltai* of 1206 and shortly thereafter. It was set down in writing in Uighur script by Shigi-Khutukhu, Genghis's literate adopted brother. Genghis made him a kind of chief justice and assigned him responsibility for maintaining the *Yasa*, instructing him to "punish the thieves and put right the lies." Many historians also name Shigi-Khutukhu as the likely author of *The Secret History of the Mongols* (c. 1240).

The *Yasa,* or code of laws, of Genghis Khan covers every conceivable aspect of tribal and army life. It prohibited lying, quarreling, interfering in the disputes and affairs of others, slavery, wife-stealing (the source of interminable warfare between tribes), and much more. The *Yasa* documented Mongol attitudes toward religious tolerance, exempted priests and religious institutions from taxation, and prescribed the death penalty for such capital offenses as spying, desertion, theft, adultery, and urinating in running water—the last because of obvious health reasons and because Mongols believed that streams and rivers brought life to the earth (just as blood coursing through veins and arteries sustained life in humans).

A FEW OF GENGHIS KHAN'S *BILIKS*

- Adulterers shall be put to death regardless of gender or marital status.
- No soldier shall leave his assigned unit; otherwise, the soldier and his commander shall be executed.
- Each Mongol tribe shall contribute to the maintenance of the khan from their annual surpluses and shall provide him with horses, rams, milk, and woolens.
- Nothing from the estate of a man who dies without heirs shall pass to the Khan; rather, his property shall pass to the person who cared for him.
- In time of peace, there shall be hunting to teach the young how to kill wild animals, to accustom them to fighting, and to build their strength and endurance so that they will later fight, without sparing themselves, against the enemy as though against wild animals.
- All religions shall be respected but preference shall be shown to none.
- The son of a deceased father may dispose of all his wives, except his mother, either by marrying them or handing them off for marriage.
- A man unable to refrain from drinking may get drunk three times a month; more than three times a month makes him culpable; twice is better, once, even more so, and not at all is best. But where is such a man to be found?
- Honor and respect the pure, the innocent, the just, the learned, and the wise of any people; despise the bad and the unjust.

Scholars first believed the *Yasa* to be proof positive of Genghis Khan's great wisdom and vision of how his future world empire should be governed. More recent thinking holds that most of the *Yasa* comprises case histories—that is, judgments rendered and retained for use as precedents in future cases. In the centuries after the great khan's reign, the *Yasa* came to include a collection of Genghis Khan's wise utterings—known as *biliks*—along with a list of Mongol customs and traditions. Because of these additions, the *Yasa* does not truly represent the cornerstone of the Mongol empire—it contains as much lore as law. The *Yasa*, in its original form, no doubt added greatly to the stability of Mongol society, but without question it was the Mongol army that defined the lives of almost all Mongols.

Beginning with his preparations for the final battle with the Naimans, Genghis Khan introduced a whole new military philosophy to the steppes. He retained the traditional concept of blood-brotherhood (*andas*) but encouraged—even emphasized—the alternate concept of devoted followers (*nokors*) who swore allegiance to their patron and proved themselves in battle to gain rewards and advancement. These *nokors* held most of the key posts in Genghis Khan's military command structure, which was conspicuously lacking the khan's blood relations.

In developing his army, Genghis Khan routinely removed traditional commanders of tribal armies and replaced them with commanders from another tribe. One Mongol *bilik* states: "If a troop commander is unable to keep his troop ready for battle, he, his wife and children will be arraigned [put on trial] and another leader will be selected from within the troop. Commanders of squadrons, regiments and divisions will be dealt with in similar manner." Genghis often broke up and scattered entire tribal armies among the ranks of other units, particularly armies with past records of unreliability. Moreover, he forbade anyone—on pain of death—to move from one unit to another without express permission. In time, the effectiveness of these methods mostly eliminated old tribal divisions and formed one strong, united army.

Genghis Khan maintained strict discipline under the direction of central authority, aimed at building cohesive units that fought as a single fighting machine and not as individuals. Those who broke the rules suffered severe punishments. His goal was to make loyalty the focus of all his men and to make himself the focus of their loyalty.

When Genghis Khan began restructuring his army, it seems unlikely that he did so with the underlying aim of conquering the world. In the past, Mongol armies justified their existence through looting and pillaging, the rewards of which enhanced their lives and those of their loved ones. A happy army makes for a controllable army. But as Genghis rose to greater and greater heights, and his army grew larger and larger, he must have recognized that restricting his operations to the Mongolian Plateau would mean less plunder to be divided between more soldiers. To keep his army happy—and thus controllable—he would have to continue to expand his circle of conquests. He could never rest on his laurels and expect to retain power.

Genghis Khan began tightening his grasp on power

by expanding the *keshig*, his elite bodyguard service, to some 10,000 men in units of one thousand, about ten times its original strength. He recruited its leaders from the sons and younger brothers of his divisional commanders, thereby reinforcing his theme of imperial loyalty. The *keshig* provided a pool of select young warriors whose advancement would be linked to the new imperial government rather than to traditional tribal affiliations. In addition to protecting the khan, this elite service would also supply hand-picked warriors for messenger and various other special duties.

Members of the *keshig* ranked above the ordinary regimental commanders, and members of their household (*kotochin*) ranked above the regular squadron and troop commanders. Genghis Khan established clear chains of command, saying, "If an ordinary regimental commander claims equality with a member of my bodyguard and quarrels with him on this score, I will punish the relevant regimental commander."

In organization of his regular army, Genghis continued to build on the decimal structure he had put in place earlier: A unit of ten men constituted an *arban*; ten *arbans*, a *jagun*, or 100 men; ten *jaguns*, a *minghan*, or 1,000 men; and ten *minghans*, a *tumen*, or 10,000 men— the equivalent of a modern army division. These units were further categorized in light and heavy cavalry groupings, with the light cavalry outnumbering heavy by about two to one. There was no Mongol infantry.

With the exception of priests, physicians, and undertakers, all men between the ages of fifteen and seventy were obligated to serve in the army. When called upon for service, they were expected to leave their flocks, gather three or four spare horses, and report to their units wherever they might be located. Wives and children either remained behind to assume the duties of their husbands and fathers, or, when the army moved abroad, they trailed behind with the family herds. Latecomers to an army on the move had no difficulty finding their way around an army camp (or *ordu*) upon arrival, since every camp was laid out in a standard pattern. The tent of the camp leader, physician, armorer, quartermaster, etc., could always be found in the same location in any camp. The quartermasters, or *jurtchis*, ran the *ordu* and were responsible for supplies and organizing the campsite.

In the Mongol army, each soldier was responsible for the upkeep of his personal clothing and equipment, and officers regularly inspected their condition to a rigid standard. A soldier's clothing started with a silk under-shirt. Tightly woven silk served as added protection against an arrow's penetration. By pulling on the silk, a physician could turn an embedded arrowhead and often remove the arrow without further damage (a technique learned from the Chinese). Next came the tunic. A light cavalryman wore little armor beyond a helmet of leather or iron, depending on his rank, although he sometimes wore a padded, quilted coat with considerable protective qualities. All cavalrymen carried a leather-covered wicker shield. A heavy cavalryman wore

A typical Mongol soldier, as depicted by Rashid al-Din. *(Bibliothèque nationale de France, Paris)*

a helmet, a coat of mail, and a cuirass (a piece of armor covering the body from the neck to the waist) made of leather-covered iron scales. John of Plano Carpini offered this description of Mongol armor in the thirteenth century: "Their cuirasses and horse armors are of leather and made this way: they take strips of cowhide or other animal hide of one hand's width wide, and they glue three or four of these together and tie them to each other with laces or cords. In the top strip they put the cords at the edge, in the one below they put them in the center and they do this until the end. Therefore, when the soldiers bend, the lower strips slide up over the upper ones and so they are doubled or even tripled over the body. . . . The Tartar [Mongol] helmet has a crown made of iron or steel, but the part that extends around the neck or throat is of leather; and all these pieces of leather are made as described above."

A few years after Carpini, the Venetian merchant and traveler Marco Polo gave a similar but less meticulous description of Mongol armor: "They wear defensive armor made of the thick hides of buffaloes and other beasts, dried by the fire, and thus rendered extremely hard and strong."

Each warrior was armed with two composite bows

This fifteenth-century illustration shows a scene from Marco Polo's travels to the Mongolian steppes in the mid-1200s where, as depicted here, he met with Kublai Khan, a descendant of Genghis Khan. *(Bibliothèque nationale de France, Paris)*

and a quiver (or quivers) containing at least sixty arrows. A light cavalryman also carried a small sword and two or three javelins. A heavy cavalryman carried a scimitar, a battle-ax or mace (a heavy, often-spiked staff or club), and a twelve-foot lance.

A Mongol soldier was expected to carry sufficient personal items and equipment on his horse (or horses) to sustain himself over the course of long campaigns. Typically, his horse(s) carried such things as clothing, cooking utensils, dried meats, a water bottle, files for sharpening arrows, needles and thread, and numerous other useful items. He carried some items in a saddlebag made from a cow's stomach. The saddlebag was inflatable and doubled as a useful float when crossing rivers and streams.

The Mongolian horse or pony—often acclaimed for its hardiness and sometimes maligned for its ugliness— held the key to the Mongol army's mobility. There is evidence that a Mongol on a single horse once covered six hundred miles in nine days. In a similarly amazing feat, Genghis Khan's army, moving nonstop, once traversed 130 miles in two days. Mongol horses knew how to dig down through snow to find food where more domesticated horses could not. The horse provided the Mongol soldier with a diet of animal products. He drank their milk, ate their flesh, and, in times of great need, even drank their blood.

This incredible mobility set the Mongol army apart from all other armies through the ages and was not equaled or surpassed until the advent of lightning war-fare in the twentieth century. The ability of Mongol ponies to live off the land wherever they went eliminated the need to carry their food, and enhanced their speed and mobility. In 1241, the emperor Frederick II, who knew a lot about Mongols and their ways of waging war, warned his fellow rulers in western Europe about the looming Mongol threat.

The Mongol soldier went to war having received unique training. A favorite training method of Genghis Khan utilized the great annual hunts called *nerge* to impart essential military skills. These hunts were held in the autumn to provide meat for the winter, but the techniques of the hunt were readily transferable to the battlefield. Teamwork, communication, and coordina-tion; the arcs and sweeps of encircling movements; and horsemanship, shooting, swordsmanship, discipline, and most importantly, obedience were instilled in these hunts. After the encirclement of the prey, the *nerge* ended with the mass slaughter of the beasts and the distribution of the game—lessons that also carried over to the battlefield.

The Mongols were the only people of the steppes to hunt in this organized and disciplined way. Some schol-ars think that Genghis Khan himself may have invented—or at least adapted—these methods to military use. Few other explanations can account for the extraordinary success of the Mongol army over less coordinated and disciplined tribes when Genghis Khan thundered across Asia in the last two decades of his life.

6

A Promise on the Mountain

After Temujin became Genghis Khan in 1206, organizational tasks took much of his time. This required his presence in camp. At first, he enjoyed a period of stability in which he delegated minor military matters to his generals and focused his attention on establishing the internal structure of his empire and consolidating the power of his ruling family. For a while, he felt no threat from beyond his borders. His nearest neighbors were stable empires and showed little interest in the internal affairs of his nation. China was then divided into three separate kingdoms. To the east, the Jurcheds had established the Chin dynasty in northern China in 1115. South of the Chin, the Sung ruled in the real heartland of China. Directly south of Mongolia, in what constitutes the western extremities of modern China, was the Tangut kingdom of Hsi Hsia (Xi Xsia). To the west of the new Mongol empire stood the domains of the Qara Khitans and their southern neighbors, the Uighurs, beyond which lay the vast lands of the northern Persian empire.

This quiet period allowed time for the first leader of all the Mongols to settle in and establish his new government. (Earlier Mongol leaders had ruled over some, or most, but never *all* Mongols.) One of his first internal problems involved the shaman Teb Tengeri, one of the seven sons of Yesugei's old servant Munlik. Many times, Teb Tengeri had claimed that God had spoken to him favorably about the rule and destiny of Genghis Khan. These pronouncements, of course, set well with Genghis, and the shaman's standing with the Mongol khan grew steadily higher. In time, however, Teb Tengeri's want of personal power became insatiable: "He was eager to

This map shows Asia as it was shortly before Genghis Khan's invasion of China.

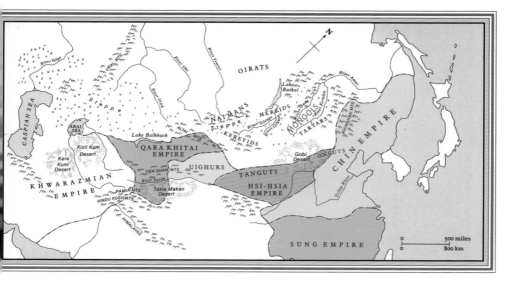

become the ruler himself." The shaman began by stirring up trouble between Genghis Khan and his brother Khasar.

One day, Teb Tengeri and his six brothers surrounded Khasar, shoved him around, and verbally abused him, intending through their actions to humiliate their ruler. When Khasar complained to his brother, Genghis Khan did not take his strong and powerful sibling seriously. He said, "You have never before allowed any person to get the better of you; how could you now permit them to triumph over you?" Khasar left embittered and did not speak to his brother for three days.

Teb Tengeri then planted a seed of suspicion in Genghis's mind when he told him of his latest revelations. On one occasion, God supposedly told the shaman that Genghis held the nation in his hands, but at other times he said the same of Khasar. Genghis Khan rode out at once and took Khasar prisoner.

Genghis apparently did not sense the threat to his rule posed by Teb Tengeri and his six brothers, but his wife Borte did. She had advised her husband when the time came to separate from Jamuka, and now she warned him that the shaman and his brothers had grown too powerful.

The next time Teb Tengeri and his brothers visited the *ger* of Genghis Khan, Temuge, one of the khan's brothers, grabbed the shaman's coat collar as if to wrestle. Genghis ordered the pair to take their differences outside.

Once outside, three of Temuge's bodyguards seized Teb Tengeri, snapped his back, and left him in a heap.

The shaman's brothers threatened Genghis Khan but his bodyguards intervened. Genghis ordered a tent to be placed over Teb Tengeri's body. Soon afterward, the corpse mysteriously disappeared. Genghis Khan explained that Teb Tengeri had dishonored his family and therefore had been punished by god. The incident permanently settled all doubt as to the dominance of imperial power over that of the priests.

While establishing his rule and settling tribal problems, Genghis often received news from Muslim traders who moved back and forth along the trade routes between the Near East and the Far East. They told many tales of the wonders and fabulous riches of the Chin Empire behind the Great Wall of China.

Genghis heard not only of the riches to be found there but also of such wondrous things as walled cities large enough to contain his entire nation, great floating buildings that sailed against currents, remarkable roads that crossed over rivers, and majestic chairs held up on poles for transporting nobles. Of even greater interest to the khan were descriptions of advanced inventions for waging war such as fire-throwing devices, great shooting stars that landed with a big bang and destroyed everything around, and huge war carts pulled by twenty or more animals.

At that time, the Chin Empire was enormously powerful. Genghis knew how the Chin had played one steppe tribe against another over the years to keep them weak and controllable. He also knew that the day would come

The Chinese began construction of the Great Wall along its border in the third century BC to keep out raiding parties. Its walls stand about thirty feet high and its towers rise to about forty feet. It still stands today and extends—in sections—for roughly 4,000 miles from the Yellow Sea to a point deep within central Asia.

when the Chin would threaten his new Mongol nation unless he struck them first. For the moment, he lacked the strength to risk a confrontation with the Chin. Genghis would first need to prepare his people for a struggle against a formidable force. The Tangut state of Hsi Hsia to the south was organized much like the two Chinas to the east, but was far weaker militarily. A campaign against the Tanguts would provide his men with perfect training for a future effort against the more powerful Chin.

In 1207, Genghis Khan launched an exploratory excursion into Hsi Hsia with some initial success but was soon caught up in a standoff at the fortified city of Wolohai (now Tingyuan) after suffering substantial

losses. Rather than return home in defeat, Genghis resorted to quick-witted trickery. He sent a message to the
Tangut commander promising to call off the Mongol
siege in return for a thousand cats and several thousand
swallows. The Tangut obliged him, whereupon Genghis
ordered his men to tie cloth streamers to the tails of the
cats and swallows, set them afire, and release them. The
terrified cats and birds instinctively streaked for home
and, upon their return, set hundreds of small fires in the
city. In the resulting confusion, the Mongols entered the
city and forced the Tanguts into submission. The Tanguts
agreed to pay a yearly tribute of costly goods and
animals. Genghis and his army went home with a minor
victory.

Back in Mongol country, Genghis reflected on the
dangers of having to rely on tricks to achieve military
aims. Fortified cities posed problems he had never faced
before. He called all of his chieftains and generals
together and established a Mongol war academy to
analyze the lessons of the battle of Wolohai. As a result
of their analyses and suggestions, Genghis added courses
in siege warfare. His men learned how to erect huge
ladders for scaling fortress walls, as well as the use of
other special equipment such as oversized shields for
protection against arrows, spears, and other missiles
launched from above. After completing their siege training, Genghis's commanders returned to their units and
began assembling great stores of weaponry, carts, shields,
and equipment, after which they continued to practice

their newly learned skills of siege warfare.

In the spring of 1209, Barchuk, the ruler of the Uighurs, sent a mission to Genghis offering to pay tribute in return for his protection. His message said: "If you, Genghis Khan, show me favor, I will be your fifth son and will place all my strength at your disposal." Genghis accepted his offer on condition that Barchuk appear before him personally "bringing gold and silver, small and large pearls, brocade, damask, and silks." Barchuk delayed his response to the khan, waiting to see what the future would bring.

That summer, Genghis, now intent on destroying Hsi Hsia, launched a major campaign against the Tangut state with an army of about 80,000 men. The campaign began with a march of about 650 miles, two hundred miles of which crossed the sandy wastes of the Gobi desert. Genghis's army met a Tangut army of 50,000 at its border and easily defeated it. They then moved on to the completely rebuilt city of Wolohai and, using their new techniques, recorded another easy triumph. Genghis next led his army across a high mountain range and through stiff Tangut resistance to lay siege to their capital city of Yinchuan on the banks of the Yellow River. He found the city surrounded by an intricate system of irrigation canals and very strongly defended. After besieging the capital for two months, Genghis was about to give up the standoff when inspiration struck him.

Genghis ordered the construction of a huge dike to

Opposite: This fourteenth-century Iranian miniature shows Genghis Khan and the Mongols making a treacherous mountain crossing in pursuit of the Chin. *(The British Museum, London)*

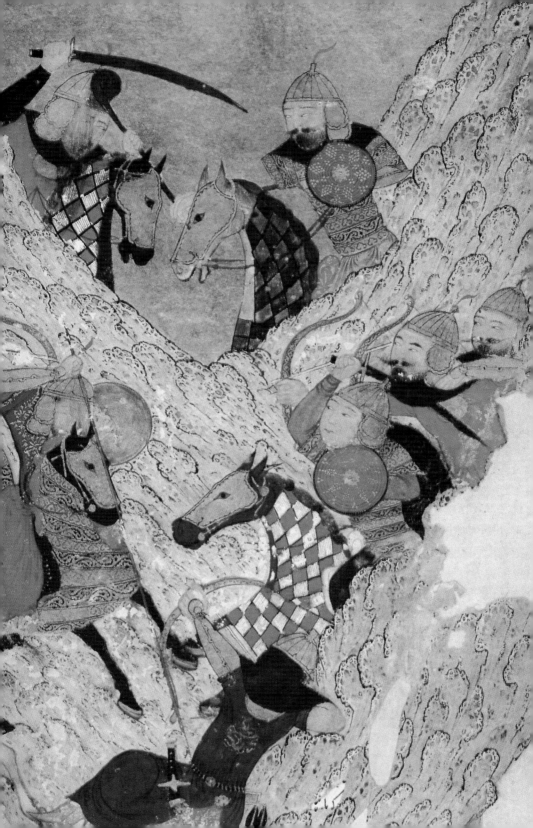

divert the waters of the Yellow River into the city. The waters soon began to flood the city. The Mongols had once again demonstrated their ability to learn fast and adapt to new and different challenges. In January of 1210, just as it appeared that the walls of Yinchuan would collapse, the dike gave way, either through faulty engineering—the Mongols were still learning—or through an action of the Tanguts to breach it. But the

When the Mongols first began to encounter fortified cities, they did not yet have advanced sieging machines and strategies, and walled cities, such as this one, proved difficult to conquer. *(Former Imperial Library of Golestan, Tehran)*

already-weakened Tanguts sued for peace terms.

Genghis demanded that the Tanguts supply him with auxiliary warriors, but the Tangut ruler answered, "We are a nation of town-dwellers. We would not be in a state to fight as auxiliaries in the event of a long march followed by a heated battle." Instead, he promised Genghis rich tribute: camels with herders, woolens and silk goods, trained falcons, and even one of his daughters as a wife to Genghis to symbolize his submission. Genghis accepted the compromise terms, but he never forgot the Tangut ruler's refusal to send auxiliary troops. He would repay the Tanguts for the slight in the years to come.

On the way home, Genghis received word from one of his messengers that the Chin emperor had died and had been succeeded by his son, Wang Wei (prince of Wei), whom Genghis detested. He had met the new ruler while serving as a mercenary for the Chin against the Tatars. Genghis considered him an idiot. A Chin envoy was already en route to the Mongol *ordu* to inform Genghis of the change of rule and to collect tribute. Genghis, the messenger said, would be expected to show his submission to the new Chin ruler by kowtowing to the east—that is, by kneeling and touching his forehead to the ground toward the Chin capital of Zhongdu (Beijing).

When Genghis arrived home and received the Chin ambassador, the envoy informed him of the change of rule. Genghis scoffed at the idea of bowing down to the Chin emperor, then he turned to the east and spat.

Genghis mounted his horse and rode off, leaving his visitors stunned. It was Genghis Khan's way of declaring war.

In the spring of 1211, Genghis called for a *khuriltai* at his base camp to prepare his followers for the coming conflict. Everyone knew the reason for the gathering. Their attendance or nonattendance would signify a yes or no vote of confidence. A poor turnout would mean Genghis could not count on enough support to wage war against the Chin. He needed the full commitment of every warrior, regardless of rank, and of everyone left behind on the home front. To keep their trust and confidence, Genghis felt it was important for them to know everything about why they were about to go to war. During the *khuriltai*, Barchuk of the Uighurs appeared, along with the Karluk chieftain, to formally recognize Genghis as their overlord. Genghis included them in the discussions. With the western Uighurs and Karluks in his fold, his rear would be protected. With Siberia to the north, which posed no threat, and the Tanguts to the south, who had severed relations with the Chin, his flanks were already secure. Strategically, Genghis was well situated for an eastward advance.

Genghis stressed three things in favor of going to war against the Jurcheds: honor, revenge, and the prospects of enormous riches in the many walled cities across the Great Wall of China. To remain a vassal of the Chin would tarnish the honor of his proud people. The time had come to seek revenge against the hated Jurcheds, who had dishonored and cruelly slain their ancestors. And if vengeance should come with treasures beyond imagination, then so much the better for the Mongol nation.

Once Genghis felt confident that he had made his case for war, and that his people and allies stood staunchly with him, he slipped out of camp alone and ascended a nearby mountain to pray. He prayed to the Eternal Blue Sky and to his supernatural guardians for three days and nights. While Genghis prayed on the mountaintop, his followers prayed and fasted in the valley—and they waited for the decision of the Eternal Blue Sky.

On the fourth day at dawn, Genghis came down off the mountain and annouced, "The Eternal Blue Sky has promised us victory and vengeance."

7

Across the Great Wall

In May of 1211, at the age of forty-nine, Genghis Khan launched his first campaign against the Chin. Until then, the world beyond Mongolia had heard little about him or the Steppe Wars. Soon, the outside world would become better informed.

Genghis's motivation was revenge, but he also needed to keep his army occupied. He could not have known it at the time, but his attack on the Chin would set in motion a conflict that would sweep across half of the known world, spawn four kingdoms, and span several generations.

Genghis chose to cross part of the Gobi desert with an army of about 65,000 men. He left a corps of 20,000 in the homeland under the command of the Unggirad Takuchar. At the time of his attack, the Chin army numbered more than 600,000, with 120,000 mounted ar-

The Gobi desert, one of the world's largest deserts, extends one thousand miles from east to west across southeast Mongolia and North China. The Gobi, located on a plateau ranging from 3,000 to 5,000 feet high, consists of a series of shallow alkaline basins. The western portion of the desert is sandy.

chers, which were the equivalent of the Mongol cavalry, and almost a half-million infantry. These figures represent the total Chin army, rather than a single force concentrated against the Mongols. If Genghis knew of his intended enemy's vastly superior numbers, he did not let it deter him.

Before beginning his 450-mile march to the Chinese border, Genghis sent a party of spies far in advance of his main army to penetrate enemy defenses and bring back captives from which to gain information. He next sent out his scouts, about two hundred horsemen, who scattered about the countryside in pairs. Their job was to check for water sources, study grass, weather, and terrain conditions, and report back. Before the main army arrived, the scouts knew every hill and gulley, every person and resource, and every avenue of retreat in the area. Far behind the scouts, Genghis dispatched his advance forces—30,000 handpicked warriors comprising three *tumens*. The *tumens* were led by the veteran Mukali, the fiery Jebe (a converted follower who once shot Genghis's horse in the shoulder with an arrow and was appropriately nicknamed the Arrow Prince), and the greatest of his generals, Subodei. Behind the vanguard, Genghis Khan always commanded the center force, and his left and right wings formed on each side of him. Genghis and each of his older sons commanded a *tumen*. The khan kept his youngest son at his side to tutor him in the art and science of war. Behind him, a small force protected his rear and brought up the reserve horses.

The Mongol army moved so fast they often did not

This detail of a painting by Rashid al-Din depicts Genghis Khan and three of his sons. *(Courtesy of Art Resource)*

SUBODEI

Students of Mongol history almost unanimously recognize Subodei as Genghis Khan's most brilliant general. Subodei was born the son of an Uriangqadai blacksmith in 1172. He was the younger brother of Jelme, one of Temujin's earliest companions. Subodei joined Temujin's band when he was about sixteen. Like his brother, he rose fast in the service of Genghis Khan and commanded cavalry at the age of twenty-five.

Subodei's first independent command came when Temujin entrusted him to pursue and kill Kutu and Chila'un, sons of the defeated Merkid leader, Tokhto'a, in 1205–1206. In the two wars against the Tangut (1207-1209) in Hsi Hsia, he commanded a *tumen* (10,000 men). In 1220, he assumed his first major command in the campaign against the Shah of the Khwarizm Empire when Genghis Khan sent him, his fellow general Jebe the Arrow, and a force of some 30,000 men in pursuit of the fleeing shah. After the shah's death in 1221, Subodei and Jebe led their forces in the first Mongol incursion into Russia, Azerbaijan, Armenia, and Georgia. Jebe died during the expedition, and Subodei led their armies back to the Mongol homeland in 1224–1225.

Subodei distinguished himself in Genghis's final campaign against the Hsi Hsia and Chin Empires and later presided over the siege and fall of the Chin Imperial capital of Kaifeng (1232-1233), after which he went on to conquer the rest of the Chin Empire. He returned to eastern Europe in 1237 and campaigned in Russia and Hungary. Subodei defeated King Bela's Hungarian army at the Sajó River in 1241, before being recalled to Mongolia upon the death of Ogodei, Genghis Khan's son and successor.

Over the years, Subodei grew so fat that the sturdy Mongolian ponies could no longer bear his weight. In later campaigns, he had to be transported to the battlefield in a cart.

Comrades and foes alike acclaimed Subodei's bold, resourceful, determined, and energetic leadership, which fully exploited the Mongol advantages of speed, mobility, and endurance. Subodei died in Mongolia in 1245 at the age of seventy-three.

pause to cook. Instead, they put raw meat beneath their saddles to soften it enough to eat. The Mongols crossed the Gobi desert in June and arrived at the Chin's outer defense ring—a string of frontier forts in front of the Great Wall. A defense force of Onghuts, who were Chin subjects, offered no resistance and allowed the Mongols to pass through without the loss of a single man. The Onghut leader was in fact a Mongol sympathizer who graciously placed a corps of 10,000 auxiliaries at Genghis's disposal.

After breaching the Chin's outer defense ring, the Mongols split up into several groups and proceeded to ravage the northern provinces of Shansi (Shanxi) and Hopeh (Hebei). With his army fragmented across North China, sometimes separated by distances of two hundred miles or more, a dependable communications system became essential to Genghis's ability to command. His "arrow messengers" (so called because they traveled as swift and straight as arrows) took care of this vital function, keeping him constantly informed about the progress in all areas. Genghis also received helpful information from oppressed and disgruntled Chin subjects.

Genghis always demanded the truth from his messengers, whether they brought good news or bad. When he got bad news, he used it to good advantage where possible, but he never punished the messenger. By contrast, when the Chin emperor in Zhongdu received bad news, he had the bearer punished. As a result, Genghis's messengers delivered the truth, while the emperor's messengers lied when their news was bad.

In another innovation introduced by Genghis, regimental commanders used black and white flags to communicate with one another and to direct the movement of their commands. At night, or when terrain features made flags difficult or impossible to see, the Mongols substituted flaming arrows to communicate.

At the outset of his campaign in China, Genghis gave priority to separating the Khitans from their Jurched rulers by effectively demonstrating the inability of the Jurcheds to protect them. And he made ample use of propaganda to win Khitan support, proclaiming his army as liberators on a mission to restore the Khitan royal family to the throne usurped by the Jurcheds a century earlier. Many Khitans, even high-ranking Chin officials, joined the Mongols. In all his campaigns, Genghis Khan exploited any internal social turmoil or rift he could find or create.

Moving deeper into Chin territory, the Mongols continued laying waste to towns and villages until they met a formidable Chin army near the Yeh-hu Mountains. Rather than retreat, Genghis decided to fight. In his first serious encounter with a foreign army, his horsemen completely outmaneuvered the Chin army in a devastating display of superiority. Within a few hours, the Mongol cavalry destroyed a force of about 70,000. Nine years later, a Taoist monk passed through the region and reported that the battlefield was still littered with human bones.

At this point, the Chin emperor made a peace proposal, sending forward a linguist who knew Genghis from an earlier visit with the Mongols. The linguist promptly defected and joined the Mongol army. Genghis gave him a command position over Mongol and Han Chinese troops. Genghis turned down the Chin emperor's peace offer.

In the autumn of 1211, Genghis took personal com-

This painting portrays the Mongol army engaged in fierce fighting with the Chin. *(Bibliothèque nationale de France, Paris)*

mand of the eastern army and headed for the strategic Juyong Pass that guarded the northern approach to Zhongdu. The Chin had attempted to strengthen the city's defenses by heavily fortifying the pass, but Jebe (the "Arrow Prince"), leading the Mongol vanguard, overcame the Chin resistance with a trick: Jebe led his attackers into the narrow corridor until he met an elite guard of Khitan and Jurched defenders. He then turned about and feigned a retreat, luring the defenders into the open when they gave chase. Genghis and the main body of cavalry then tore into the defenders and annihilated them.

John of Plano Carpini described the Mongol (Tartar) fighting techniques this way: "[W]hen the Tartars see the enemy they advance and everyone shoots three of four arrows, and if they see that they cannot overwhelm the enemy they go back to their comrades. And this is a trick, so that their adversaries follow them to a place where the Tartars have prepared an ambush. If their enemies follow them to this trap, the Tartars circle around them and wound them and kill them. If the Tartars see that the enemy is very numerous, they sometimes turn away for a day or two and invade and despoil a different area and kill men and lay waste the country. If they find they cannot do this, they sometimes retreat for ten or twelve days and stay in a safe place until their adversaries' army disbands and then they secretly come and depopulate the entire country."

After "depopulating" the Juyong Pass, Genghis and

his horde rode through the narrow corridor and onto the plains surrounding Zhongdu, where they continued their plundering but made no attempt to lay siege to the capital.

In November and December of 1211, Ila Ahai, a member of the ruling house of the Khitans who had joined Genghis at Baljuna, dealt another serious blow to the Chin. He and his forces conducted a series of raids into the imperial pasturelands containing the reserve horses of the Chin and drove them off, thereby depriving their cavalry of their main source of spare mounts. By early 1212, the lower altitude, moist climate, and a variety of lowland maladies had begun to toll on the Mongols, and they withdrew to winter quarters at Dolon Nor (Seven Lakes, now Duolon), on the cooler elevations of the Inner Mongolia grasslands.

After his first campaign against the Chin, which had gained him very little, Genghis recognized that the real riches of the East lay within the walled cities. He also realized that his army was still poorly prepared to breach the defenses of the stone fortresses. The Mongol army spent the next several months practicing new techniques of siege craft devised by Genghis and a staff of skilled Chinese engineers who had defected and joined him. Genghis refined old siege weapons and added new ones to his arsenal: the catapult for hurtling massive stones, flaming liquids, or other lethal substances at or

Opposite: The Mongols devised huge catapults, such as the one shown in this painting, to attack the Chinese fortified cities that had once been impenetrable. *(Edinburgh University Library)*

احكام نوابه نع ملك الاعمال نو يُوك ال الاسقاص لجب
ابنه الامير ضرن من ناصر الدين والتونشاش الحاجب وابو عـ
منتصف ذى الحجة سنه ثلث و تسعين و تلئمانة بعد سايه من

over city walls; the trebuchet, a catapult operated by the release of a heavy counterweight that propelled missiles faster and farther than tension- or torsion-powered catapults; and the ballista, a form of crossbow for launching huge arrows or other missiles. These weapons and others became a permanent part of the Mongol arsenal.

In early 1212, Genghis's appeal to the subjugated Khitans to rise up against their oppressors drew a response from a descendant of the Khitan royal family named Liuge. He amassed an army of 100,000 men and revolted against the Chin in the Liao River region (northeast China). Genghis, in apparent anticipation of the event, sent Jebe to help Liuge seize the strongly defended city of Liaoyang. Jebe, recognizing that he stood little chance of capturing the city with cavalry alone, resorted again to deception. After a halfhearted assault on the city, he feigned retreat, leaving a vast store of military supplies behind at the gate to the city. That night, while the defenders were retrieving the supplies, Jebe returned with his cavalry. They came in through the open gate and seized the city without a fight. Liuge declared himself *du yuanshuai* (supreme commander) of Liaodong peninsula, created a new Liao Empire, and swore allegiance to Genghis Khan. He served Genghis loyally until his death in 1220. Liuge's part in the defeat of the Chin was yet another example of Genghis's ability to attract followers.

Genghis launched his second campaign against the Chin in the spring of 1212. His winter sojourn had allowed the Chin time to reclaim and refortify lost territories. The Mongols, probably because of their limited numbers, had made no effort to occupy lands they had conquered earlier. This time, Genghis enjoyed more success at capturing walled cities, typically using the siege techniques described by John of Plano Carpini: "[I]f a place is well fortified they surround it and securely hedge it in so that no one can get in or out, and they fight fiercely with machines and arrows and do [not] stop the attack by day nor night, so that those in the fort can not rest. The Tartars do rest however, because they divide up their battalions and one follows the other in fighting so they are not tired at all. If they cannot take the place that way, they throw Greek fire [incendiary material]. In fact, they sometimes take the grease of the men they kill and throw it liquefied onto the houses, and wherever the grease catches fire it burns as though it cannot be extinguished. Yet it may be put out, they say, by pouring wine or beer over it, and if it falls onto flesh it may be extinguished by rubbing it with the palm of the hand."

Carpini goes on to describe tunneling under the fortification as an alternate way of gaining entry. Sometimes the Mongols tried to persuade their besieged enemies to surrender, but Carpini offered words of caution for those inclined to give themselves up to Mongols: "In their wars they kill whomever they capture, unless by chance they decide to keep them as slaves. They assign those to be killed to captains of hundreds so they may be killed by them with battle axes; these captains then divide the captives as they decide and give ten or more or less to a servant to be killed."

Genghis often killed the ruling classes of the people he conquered to eliminate their leadership and to keep the people docile, but he usually spared most of the people so long as they agreed to observe his laws and live in peace as loyal subjects. He always culled the ranks of the conquered for professional people and craftsmen who could serve him well. Woe befell anyone who crossed him, however, for Genghis thought nothing of wiping out entire cities of dissenters.

In August of 1212, the string of Mongol successes was abruptly halted when Genghis laid siege to the Chin's western capital of Xijing (Datong) and was struck by an arrow. The wound forced him to turn over command of his armies while he went north again to recuperate. While Genghis convalesced, the Jurcheds regained most of their lost territory, including the Juyong Pass. When hostilities resumed in the autumn of 1213, however, the Mongols regained the strategic pass with the help of Ja'far, a Muslim trader who had also joined Genghis at Baljuna. Ja'far knew of a secret path that enabled the Mongol army to slip through in darkness and slaughter a garrison of sleeping defenders at Juyong Pass.

Opposite: This battle scene, painted in the sixteenth century, shows the Mongols using sophisticated equipment, such as cannons, to fight their enemy. *(Courtesy of Art Resource.)*

The Mongols resumed their pattern of raiding and plundering, operating in highly mobile but coordinated advances. Jurched defections abounded, and Genghis formed fifty-six brigades of former Chin officers and men. Reinforced, the hordes of Genghis Khan sacked some ninety flourishing cities. They at last reaped the riches they had come for—gold and silver, silks and satins, male and female captives, horses and other animals, and much more. Only nine cities defended themselves sufficiently to escape ruination.

In the spring of 1214, the Mongols controlled much of the Chin empire. Genghis deployed his army in front of the capital, Zhongdu, with his left wing under his brothers Khasar and Temuge-Otchigen and his right wing under his sons Jochi, Chagatai, and Ogodei. At the same time, Mukali led an expedition into the Liaodong peninsula in northeast China to repel a Jurched countermove and to recapture the city of Liaoyang. The expedition afforded the Mongols their first glimpse of the ocean. Then two things happened to alter the situation profoundly.

First, internal problems—disunity, famine, and disease—continued to plague the Chinese. The Chin troubles came to a head when the Jurched general Hushahu, who commanded a powerful private army, defected to the Mongols. Hushahu's desertion enabled Genghis to breach the Jijing (Xijing) Pass near the western capital, where the Mongols killed many more Jurcheds. Hushahu, an extremely ambitious man, made his way to Zhongdu (where his defection was not yet known), assassinated the emperor, Wang Wei, and installed Wei's nephew on the Chin throne as Emperor Xuan-zang.

Second, the Mongols themselves were beginning to feel the effects of famine and disease, and their situation soon became desperate. According to Carpini, "The siege was so extended that the armies' provisions were completely exhausted; because they had nothing left to eat Genghis Khan had to order the sacrifice of every tenth man in order to provide sustenance for his comrades." His generals—who were well aware of the riches within the walls of Zhongdu—urged Genghis to end the standoff and attack the city, but Genghis decided instead to begin peace talks with the Chin.

Genghis put the Muslim trader Ja'far in charge of conducting peace negotiations and sent this message to the new Chin emperor: "Your districts and counties in Shandong and Hebei are now in my possession, leaving you with only [Henan]. Heaven has so weakened you that, if I was also now to attack you in your distress, what would Heaven think of me? I therefore intend to turn back with my army. Might you not provide some supplies for my troops, thus lessening the resentment of my generals?"

The Chin emperor was glad to be able to lavish gifts upon the Mongols to be rid of them. In return for peace, he gave Genghis Khan a princess as his wife, five hundred boy slaves and an equal number of girl slaves,

3,000 horses, and untold quantities of gold, silver, silk, brocades, and other valuables. The Mongols "took away from Zhongdu as much as they could carry." Genghis then retired to his temporary camp in the north. But the peace purchased at great cost by the Chin emperor resulted in little more than a temporary ceasefire.

In the summer of 1214, the emperor, figuring Zhongdu was a little too close to the northern passes leading to Mongolia, moved his imperial residence to the southern capital of Kaifeng, south of the Yellow River. The emperor's subjects took his move as a sign of cowardice and began to revolt. When Genghis heard the news of the emperor's move, he interpreted it as a breach of trust. He worried the emperor did not intend to honor the peace agreement.

Genghis had reason to feel concerned. The Chin's southern capital lay to the far side of the river where the Mongols had halted their southward drive. The Yellow River represented an almost insurmountable barrier to an army lacking engineering resources. Further, the Chin withdrawal could indicate their intention of re-building their strength in safety, while waiting for the right time to move northward again to recover their

China's great Yellow River stretches 3,000 miles.

This modern Mongol Chinese painting shows Genghis Khan's carriage stuck in the mud, an event that is rumored to have happened near the Yellow River.

losses. Genghis resumed the siege of Zhongdu in the autumn of 1214.

The Mongols returned with a larger army, well equipped and prepared to stay as long as it took to capture the city. A twenty-six-mile-long wall with twelve heavily guarded gates surrounded Zhongdu, one of the largest cities of the thirteenth century. The wall stood forty feet high, measuring forty feet wide at the top and fifty feet wide at the base. Outside the wall, three moats surrounded the city, along with nine hundred towers brimming with soldiers, and four well-positioned forts.

As the months wore on and the Mongol siege held fast, the people of Zhongdu suffered terrible deprivations and even resorted to cannibalism to survive. Zhongdu finally fell in May 1215. The Chin commanders abandoned the city, and the Mongols entered unopposed. The Mongols, frustrated by many months of denied access and driven by a need to set an example to others of what happens to those who resist them, burned and sacked the city in a month-long bloodbath. Because of their small numbers compared to the much more heavily populated nations surrounding them, the Mongols relied in great degree on mass slaughter, or the threat of it, to keep control over the lands and peoples of their conquests. In the case of Zhongdu, the threat became real. Of the carnage in Zhongdu, Persian historian Nasir al-Din Juzjani writes: "When a few years later Baha ad-Din, leader of a mission from Sultan Muhammad of [Khwarizm], approached the capital he saw a white hill and in answer to his query was told by the guide that it consisted of the bones of the massacred inhabitants. At another place the earth was, for a long stretch of the road, greasy from human fat and the air was so polluted that several members of the mission became ill and some died. This was the place, they were told, where on the day the city was stormed 60,000 virgins threw themselves to death from the fortifications in order to escape capture by the Mongols." This tale probably grew in the telling, but stories such as this one preceded the Mongols wherever they went. As skilled as the Mongols were at the art of war, they were at least as crafty in the art of propaganda.

After the fall of Zhongdu, innumerable Chin, Chinese, and Khitan troops swung their allegiance to Genghis Khan, along with many administrators and officials responsible for governing the northern part of the Chin empire. Of all the treasures drawn from Zhongdu, perhaps none was so valuable as a Khitan captive named Yelü Chucai, a young man in his twenties, who was also a member of the Khitan royal family. The young man won the Mongol leader's respect and confidence with his display of honesty, loyalty, and bravery, virtues that Genghis admired most.

Yelü Chucai added wisdom to his show of virtues when he pointed out that the new Mongol empire could be won through fighting but could not be maintained that way. Genghis recognized in the young Khitan the one he needed to administer his ever-expanding empire. Yelü Chucai would become an eminent statesman and serve as Genghis's administrator, court astrologer-astronomer, and intellectual advisor.

Genghis returned to his homeland in the spring of 1216. The following year, he appointed Mukali his viceroy (representative and governor) in the east with orders to destroy the rest of the Chin power. Mukali—with eight concubines and an all-female orchestra whose music he liked listening to while dining—campaigned up and down the Yellow River basin against the Chin for the next twenty years, before he finally died of exhaustion.

Meanwhile, in 1217, Genghis Khan turned his attention to the west. Guchlug, the son of Tayang Khan and Genghis's old adversary, had risen to a position of power among the Qara Khitans and was stirring up trouble again.

West of the Moon

When Genghis Khan returned from campaigning against the Chin, long caravans of riches of every sort followed him to Khodoe Aral. To those who had stayed at home, it must have seemed as if the storied Silk Road had been diverted northward in a glittering river of silks, satins, brocade, brass pots, bronze knives, and perfumes; jewelry crafted from precious metals and set with pearls, emeralds, and diamonds; skins of wine, casks of honey, bricks of tea, and more. Genghis had long been aware of the steady flow of opulence that caravanned back and forth along the Silk Road to the south, carrying the best of the East and West for exchange. The road started in Shansi province and stretched 4,000 miles to the Mediterranean Sea, forming a living link between two great civilizations. He knew from personal experi-

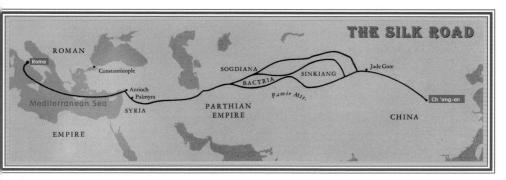

This map shows the route of the legendary 4,000-mile-long Silk Road.

ence about the lands that lay to the east. His thoughts now began to turn toward the great empire to the west of Qara Khitai called Khwarizm. But first he had some problems at home that needed his attention.

Some of the tribes Genghis had conquered earlier used his absence as a good time to quit paying tribute. When the khan returned to the region, he made it a priority to remind each and every tribe of their obligation to him and his treasury. The loyalty of his people was always at stake.

The khan's most worrisome problem lay in the west with Guchlug, the son of the deceased Tayang Khan of the Naiman. After his defeat in 1208 at Chakirma'ut, near the Irtysch River, Guchlug had fled to Qara Khitai. He later married one of the daughters of the Qara Khitan ruler and usurped his power. Under his wife's influence, Guchlug converted from his Nestorian religion to her Buddhist faith. Both Christian and Buddhist subjects of Qara Khitai shared a common mistrust of the Uighur subjects who were Muslim. Guchlug used his newly acquired power to persecute the Uighurs and limit their rights to practice their religion. The Muslims appealed to Genghis Khan for help.

Genghis, who believed that every religion should be respected, sent Jebe with 20,000 men 2,500 miles across the steppes to aid the Muslims. The potential threat of Guchlug's growing power to Genghis's rule might also have had something to do with the khan's decision. When Jebe caught up with Guchlug, he cut off his head and carried it back as proof of his success. Also, as a gift for Genghis Khan, Jebe brought back one thousand of the highly prized white-muzzled horses of Qara Khitai to make up for the horse his arrow had shot out from under Genghis several years earlier.

About 1217, while Jebe was chasing Guchlug, Genghis sent three envoys to Muhammad II, Shah of Khwarizm, ostensibly to explore his feelings about establishing a trade agreement. Along with his ambassadors, he sent lavish gifts of gold, jade, ivory ornaments, and cloaks woven from the wool of white camels. His envoys delivered the gifts with a cagy letter: "I have the greatest desire to live in peace with you. I shall look on you as my son. For your part, you are not unaware that I have conquered North China and subjected all the tribes of the north. You know that my country is an ant heap of warriors, a mine of silver, and that I have no need to covet other dominions. We have an equal interest in fostering trade between our subjects."

Because of the ambiguous wording of the letter, its

true intent is unclear. It is possible that Genghis, now in his mid-fifties, was beginning to think about abandoning military campaigns. But calling the shah his son could be considered an insult in the diplomatic language of the time and place, which would be a clear provocation for a war.

If Genghis had truly been planning to attack the shah, his reluctance to make his move in 1218 was understandable. He had just come off a long campaign, and his forces were stretched thin across half of Asia. By contrast, Muhammad II had inherited a vast empire that began in present-day Uzbekistan. With a 400,000-man army in Transoxiana alone, he expanded his domain to include most of what is now Iran, Afghanistan, and Pakistan. The shah was not much of a general himself, but his son, Jalal al-Din, possessed a natural command ability, which he would soon demonstrate against the Mongols.

Genghis Khan sent a Mongol trading caravan into the Khwarizm territories to begin trade relations. The caravan consisted of about 450 traders—mostly Muslim and Hindu merchants—and carried great quantities of luxury items, including Chinese silks, silver bars, raw jade, pieces of art made by Chinese craftsmen, furs, and bolts of white camel cloth. To purchase Khwarizmian trade goods, the khan's personal representative carried a goodly sum of money and a cordial letter from Genghis to Muhammad II, encouraging trade so that "henceforth the abscess of evil thoughts may be lanced by the improvement of relations and agreement between us, and the pus of sedition and rebellion removed."

When the caravan entered Otrar, the northeastern province of Khwarizm (now part of Kazakhstan), the greedy and arrogant provincial governor, Inal Khan, seized the trade goods and killed the merchants and their drivers. The governor did not realize it then, but far more than wiping out a caravan, he had "laid waste a whole world."

Surprisingly, Genghis Khan controlled his anger when he learned of the caravan's fate. He sent three envoys to the court of Muhammad II demanding reparations. The shah answered by killing the chief Mongol ambassador. He then burned the beards off the faces of the other two envoys and sent them back to Genghis in humiliation. This was a clear invitation to meet on the battlefield. Mongols always treated the ambassadors of other nations with great respect and expected the same in return. Genghis first wept at the death of his emissary, then raged at the shah's insult: "The [shah] is no king, he is a bandit!" he exclaimed. "If he were a king he would not have killed my merchants and my envoys who went to Otrar. Kings do not kill envoys!"

Then, as Genghis had done so many times before, he climbed to the top of a hill, lifted his face to the Eternal Blue Sky, and prayed for three days. When he came down off the hill, he began preparations for war.

Genghis called a *khuriltai* to plan his campaign. He proclaimed new laws and issued orders for conducting

Ogodei Khan.

the impending campaign. One of his wives, Yesui the Tatar, suggested to her fifty-six-year-old husband that he should name a successor. Traditionally, succession passed to the eldest son. But because Jochi's paternity had long been in question, Chagatai, the next in line, raised strident objections to his elder brother as successor. After a spirited family discussion, Genghis named Ogodei, his third and most universally liked son, as his successor. That settled, the Mongols went to war.

Genghis Khan was already master of the eastern half of the Asian continent. He began his campaign to conquer the western half in 1219. He took his wife Hulan with him and left his youngest brother, Temuge-Otchigen, in charge of his home headquarters. In his preparations he had gathered some 200,000 warriors from all four corners of his empire. It was the largest Mongol army

ever assembled, but it was still less than half the size of
Muhammad's army. With 200,000 mounted horsemen,
several hundred thousand spare horses, and a huge siege
train—complete with catapults, flamethrowers, batter-
ing rams, and the like—Genghis headed toward
Transoxiana, the setting sun, and other vast regions west
of the moon.

Transoxiana's four sides are bounded by the Oxus
(Amu Darya) and the Jaxartes (Syr Darya) rivers, the
Aral Sea, and the Pamir massif. Together, they form a
rough rectangle jutting outward from Iran into the central Asian steppes, with the wastes of the Kyzyl Kum
desert at its center. In the northwest corner of the rectangle, just south of the Aral Sea, stood the Khwarizm
district and its capital, Urgench, from which the shah's
empire had blossomed. The city of Otrar, where Inal
Khan had intercepted Genghis's caravan, lay due east of
Urgench on the Jaxartes River. At the south end of the
rectangle stood the cities of Bukhara, Khojend, and
Samarkand. And to the west of Transoxiana, between the
Oxus River and central Iran, lay the larger area of
Khorasan, another parched zone dotted with cities en-
riched by diligently cared for irrigation canals—Termez,
Balkh, Herat, Bamian, Merv, Nishapur, and more. The
Mongols would visit them all.

Genghis divided his forces into four main armies,
commanded by himself and three of his sons: Jochi,
Chagatai, and Ogodei. He sent Jochi and Jebe to the
south as diversionary forces. To the north, Chagatai and

Ogodei moved past Lake Balkash in parallel columns of some 50,000 men each to attack Otrar on the Jaxartes River. Genghis, with Subodei and an army of like size, skirted wide to the north and seemed to disappear—at least from the tracking eyes of the shah's spies.

In March 1220, Genghis emerged west of Bukhara, some four hundred miles behind enemy lines. With the aid of a guide, he had led his army on a secret route through the hazardous Kyzyl Kum desert—which the shah had thought impassable—and was bearing down fast on Bukhara.

In the meantime, Muhammad II, near Samarkand, learned of Jebe's alarming advance into the interior. He quickly moved some 100,000 men to the southeast to secure his communication lines to Khorasan and Ghazni (now in east Afghanistan). Then he received the stunning, totally unexpected news that Genghis Khan himself was rapidly approaching Bukhara. In the face of the swift Mongol advance and the havoc they were leaving behind, the Khwarizmians greatly overestimated the strength of the Mongols. Believing the Mongol numbers to exceed his own forces of a half million, Muhammad II panicked. Instead of concentrating his forces, he scattered all his available legions into Bukhara, Samarkand, and other fortresses.

At Bukhara, when the people sighted the Mongol army, it was too late. Genghis entered the city and rode right into its largest mosque, thinking it was the shah's palace. When he learned of his mistake, he ascended the pulpit and admonished the people for the treachery of their shah. "I am the punishment of God," he informed them. "If you had not committed great sins, he would not have sent a punishment like me." To spread fear across the land, Genghis allowed most of the Bukhara's population to escape, then ordered the methodical slaughter of the city's remaining 30,000 inhabitants. Afterward, the Mongols sacked the city and burned it to the ground.

While Genghis was razing Bukhara, his sons sacked and destroyed Khojend and Otrar, and Jebe defeated an army thrown against him by the shah. In accord with Genghis Khan's orders, the governor of Otrar, Inal Khan, and his wife were captured alive. Inal Khan was later executed in Samarkand by having molten silver poured into his eyes and ears.

Genghis left Bukhara and moved east to Samarkand, one of the great commercial cities of the world, where he joined the rest of his forces outside the city. The Mongols expected Samarkand—where Muhammad II had moved his capital—to withstand their assault for as long as a year; it fell in five days. The Turkish garrison of some 30,000 men mounted a brave attempt to fend off the Mongols using elephants, but the Mongol archers foiled their efforts.

The Mongols then stormed Samarkand and began to pillage the city. They offered safety to those who chose not to resist or hide, but killed anyone who violated

Opposite: In this fourteenth-century Persian miniature, Genghis Khan berates the citizens of Bukhara at the city's Great Mosque. *(The British Museum, London)*

بر مسجد بخارا را

ولم حست سیدبیرسس سما
شما داست تادان جهانم
جواد خزان جزخزآنم
بسونم پکبادکی خشک ت
نرید پرند ازتاب آن
اکر مسجد ازمانفه سود

دراد بید دمم زهر سما
زه دربندابن ام بداہتم
بزدندقربان من آمدم
برا دانم ازکده ره ببقم ب
درآن روز بردشت بان
پکبار ه آتش باآوخشد

مرا هرکزازین سقر ہرہ لکش
کشیذند شیس بران سیاه
برکش جز جزمون کذت

بوآیت جوآش سیدم زد
سدوی یکتی زآتش سیا
ان سایه پدوده شدآنآں

روز باشد سیا
یک رویه ا
مه بہ سمن
رخ کشگ
ت کشت زرخا

their terms on the spot. Soon, only a few remained to resist.

After the fall of Samarkand, Genghis evacuated the city until his men had thoroughly pillaged it. He then took about three hundred craftsmen into his ranks and permitted the remaining survivors to return to the city.

Muhammad II evaded capture at Samarkand. After naming his son, Jalal al-Din, as his successor, the shah fled south to the city of Balkh with his family and a small bodyguard. Genghis sent two of his best generals after the shah to kill him. He died of natural causes before they caught him.

After Samarkand, Genghis Khan consolidated his forces and oversaw the "cleanup" work of his sons Jochi, Chagatai, and Ogodei in Khwarizm, then looked on as his youngest son Tolui rampaged across Khorasan. Muslim resistance held on stubbornly—but in the end for nothing—at Herat, Merv, and Bamian.

At Bamian, in the west end of the Hindu Kush mountain range, one of Genghis's favorite grandsons was struck and killed by a square-headed arrow. His death brought the wrath of the Great Khan down upon the city. He ordered every inhabitant put to death.

Meanwhile, Genghis's spies and arrow messengers brought news that Jalal al-Din, a much better general than his father the shah, was raising a new army in Ghazni. While still gathering together the armies of his four sons for another campaign, Genghis sent an advance, 30,000-man contingent to seek out and engage the new Turkish army. Jalal al-Din, with an army of about 120,000 men, defeated the Mongol contingent in the Hindu Kush. Genghis acted swiftly to move with force against the Turk, whose army was diminished after his battle with the Mongols. Jalal al-Din withdrew into the northern Punjab (now part of Pakistan) with 30,000 men. Genghis followed with about 50,000.

Genghis caught up with the Turk just as he was about to cross the Indus River into India. The Mongols encircled the smaller Turkish force on three sides and forced Jalal al-Din to fight, which he did until the Mongols destroyed his army around him. The heroic young shah saved himself only by stripping himself of his armor and riding his horse off a twenty-foot cliff into

In 1222, Genghis Khan, perhaps sensing that the end of his life was nearing, took an interest in spirituality and ideas of immortality, and summoned Taoist master Ch'ang-ch'un, who traveled across Asia by carriage to consult with the Mongol leader.

the Indus, then swimming in a hail of Mongol arrows to the far shore.

Genghis watched his adversary's escape in admiration and held up Jalal al-Din's courage as an example for his own men to follow. His admiration did not stop him from sending a few *tumens* after Jalal al-Din, however. The pursuers ravaged the Lahore, Peshawar, and Multan districts of the Punjab but failed to catch up with the fleeing shah. Jalal al-Din, a man without a country, became a bandit and a renegade adventurer in Afghanistan. He was later murdered there in 1231.

After the death of Muhammad II, Jebe and Subodei made plans to return home. With permission from Genghis, they took the long way. They rode around the south of the Caspian Sea, laying waste to the Armenians and Georgians in their path, then crossed through the Caucasus Mountains and on to the great steppes, destroying Russian and Kipchak armies sent against them. In 1224, Genghis summoned his two superlative generals by courier, and they swung past the north of the Caspian Sea and headed east to rejoin their leader. Jebe fell ill and died along the way, but Subodei led their armies home, completing a fighting journey of about 4,000 miles in three years. The well-traveled general brought Genghis a wealth of valuable information about the Crimea and southern Russia. The khan's sons would put that information to good use two decades later.

Jochi, the khan's oldest son, elected to remain in the newly conquered territory. He died in 1225 at the age of forty under mysterious circumstances—possibly poisoned by his own father. Jochi did not get along with Chagatai, and it is possible that Genghis feared his own death might give rise to armed conflict between his two oldest sons. He may have ordered Jochi's death to ensure the future stability of his empire.

The defeat of Jalal al-Din essentially ended Genghis Khan's campaign in the vast regions west of the moon. Genghis stayed for some time in Afghanistan. He later wintered in Samarkand and sojourned in Tashkent, north of the Jaxartes River, in the summer of 1223. Genghis spent the summer after that on the upper Irtysch River before commencing the last leg of his homeward journey. He arrived at Khodoe Aral in 1225.

Upon his return, Genghis learned that the Tanguts of Hsi Hsia and the Jurcheds of the Chin dynasty had reestablished relations and were even then conspiring to recover the lands they had lost to him. Almost before the sweat dried on his horses, Genghis began to prepare for his last campaign.

9

Death and Legacy

In 1226, Genghis, at the head of a great Mongol army of 180,000 men, set out once again on a punitive campaign. This time, he took with him his Tangut wife Yesui, his sons Ogodei and Tolui, his chancellor Yelü Chucai, his old and steadfast companion Boorchu, and the brilliant veteran general Subodei. His son Chagatai remained behind in Mongolia. The impending campaign was to become one of the briefest—but bloodiest—Mongol expeditions.

Genghis and his horde entered Hsi Hsia and, as they had done in the Chin and Khwarizm empires, proceeded to devastate everything in their path. Somewhere along the way to the Tangut capital of Yinchuan (Ningxia), Genghis participated in a hunt for wild horses and took a bad fall when his roan panicked and threw him. Back

Genghis Khan loved to hunt and eventually died of an injury he sustained while hunting for wild horses. In this image, painted on silk, he is pictured on a falcon hunt. *(Kabul Museum)*

at his *ordu*, physicians discovered that he had suffered a number of serious injuries and pleaded with him to return home to recuperate. The khan refused on grounds that the Tanguts would interpret a withdrawal as a sign of weakness. Genghis hid his pain from his warriors, and the campaign continued.

The Mongols swarmed over several cities and were approaching the Tangut capital by the end of 1226. The Tanguts, thinking to take advantage of the wintery conditions, sent a formidable force to meet the Mongols at the iced-over Yellow River, and a great battle ensued. As the Mongols so often did, they outfoxed their hardcharging opponents. While the Tangut horses with iron shoes slipped and slid as they advanced, the Mongol horses moved about stably with felt-covered hooves on ice that the Mongols had sanded over with grit. While the Tangut horses skidded and crashed into one another, falling and throwing their riders, the Mongols systematically picked off their enemies with their arrows. The victorious Mongols went on to lay siege to the Tangut capital.

Genghis left a siege corps at Yinchuan and then moved on to the south, sacking cities and eventually setting up a base camp in Shensi province to perpetuate his looting and razing of cities in the surrounding region.

The Mongol campaign against the Tangut ended in August 1227. Only a few days before the fall of Yinchuan, Genghis summoned his sons Ogodei and Tolui to his *ger*. When they arrived, they found him wrapped in blankets and shivering by a small fire. He rocked in pain and ranted in delirium, prosphesying that his descendants would forget all he gave them.

Genghis rallied enough to instruct Tolui how to complete the campaign. He made his sons pledge to continue the war against the Chin, and then the three warriors discussed how to wage the campaign in China. Lastly, Genghis extracted a promise from his sons to kill the Tangut king and all the inhabitants of his capital.

Genghis Khan, ruler of the Mongols and of all the world he knew, died sometime in August 1227. His passing came at the age of sixty-five, probably somewhere in the Ordos (Mu Us), a high-desert region in Inner Mongolia. In accordance with the khan's instructions, his closest followers kept his death secret until the fall of Yinchuan. When the Tanguts capitulated and swung open the gates of their capital, the Mongol soldiers were finally told of Genghis's death. With drawn swords, the Mongols stormed through the gates. They killed the Tangut king and slaughtered every living thing in the city.

The Great Khan's Tatar wife Yesui oversaw the preparation of his body for burial. Attendants cleansed and dressed him in the simple clothes he was accustomed to wearing: a plain white robe, felt boots, and a hat. His body was wrapped in a white felt blanket disinfected with sandalwood, the aromatic, multipurpose wood of the Orient that freshens the air and turns away insects. A felt coffin bound with three golden straps completed their preparations.

On the third day, a procession of a thousand nobles and their warriors gathered around a simple cart bearing

This image by Rashid al-Din depicts the elaborate funeral service of Genghis Khan in 1227. *(Bibliothèque nationale de France, Paris)*

the Great Khan's body and set out for Mongolia. The Spirit Banner of Genghis Khan led the procession, followed by a female shaman, the khan's riderless horse, and the cart drawn by fifteen oxen. Along the way, the mourners surrounded the cart to shield Genghis's body from the view of onlookers. As they journeyed over mountains, through forests, and across deserts and streams, the Mongols observed absolute silence. In accordance with tradition, the Mongols killed every person and animal in their path to ensure secrecy and to provide chattel for the deceased in the afterworld.

Opposite: This sixteenth-century Indian Mughal painting depicts a popular legend about the funeral of Genghis Khan in which his funeral procession was marked by the murder of all those who attended it. *(The British Library, London)*

Genghis Khan, as he had requested, was buried on Burkhan Khaldun ("God Mountain"), the sacred mountain that rises near the three rivers of Onon, Kerulen, and Tuul. Forty jeweled slave girls and forty of the finest horses were sacrificed and buried alongside him. After his burial, a thousand horsemen rode over his gravesite to disguise its location, and the steppes reclaimed the site with fresh undergrowth within a generation. Its exact location remains unknown to this day.

Genghis Khan had unified his nation, introduced order to the steppes, fused an irresistible army, and set his people on a path to world dominion. At the Great Khan's death, the Mongol Empire extended east from the Black Sea to the Sea of Japan and south to the Arabian Sea, where it followed the Indus River to the northeast and then stretched eastward across China to the Yellow Sea. As Genghis had predicted, it fell to his sons—and to his grandsons—to further expand the empire. By 1242, Mongols had conquered as far west as Austria and Germany. A decade later, the empire included Iran, Iraq, and Syria.

The sons of Genghis Khan kept their promise and marched against both the Chin and the Sung dynasties, and conquered all of China. Kublai Khan, Tolui's son, became the emperor of China in 1260 and ruled until his death in 1294. The vast Mongol Empire began to fragment upon his death, although the Golden Khanate, which covered most of European Russia and reached eastward deep into Siberia at its peak, flourished until 1480.

This silk portrait is the only known thirteenth-century painting of Genghis Khan, created thirty years after his death. *(National Palace Museum, Taipei)*

Genghis Khan will likely always be remembered best for the havoc he wrought and the blood he spilled. At the same time, however, his generalship has seldom been equaled—and perhaps has never been surpassed—in the long history of human conflict. He should also be recalled in company with great generals such as Alexander the Great and Napoleon. To his sons and to his people, he left not only a grand empire but also the

The Mongol empire in 1300. *(Library of Congress)*

rules and laws to effectively govern it, thereby enabling it to endure and expand.

In the course of his conquests, Genghis Khan routinely oversaw the slaughter of sophisticated populations and the destruction of their cultural achievements— shining cities rising out barren deserts, museums filled with masterful works of art, and libraries replete with the wonders of science, mathematics, and fine literature— all irreplaceable. Conversely, his conquests opened wide the door to trade and cultural exchange between the East and West.

Undeniably, Genghis Khan was ruthless and cruel toward his enemies; he was also gentle and kind toward his friends. Like his life, the legacy of Genghis Khan remains a study in contrasts.

Timeline

1162   Approximate date of birth of Temujin (Genghis Khan).

1171   Temujin is betrothed to Borte, a member of the Unggirad tribe; Temujin's father dies of poisoning; the Tayichiud tribe abandons his family.

1173   Temujin and Jamuka, of the Jadaran tribe, twice become sworn brothers (*anda*).

1177   Temujin and Khasar kill their half brother Begter; Tayichiud tribe captures Temujin but he soon escapes.

1178   Temujin and Borte are married; he cultivates an alliance with Torghil, leader of the Kereyid tribe.

1179   Borte abducted by a Merkid raiding party; Temujin—allied with Torghil and Jamuka—mounts an expedition against the Merkids and recovers Borte; she soon gives birth to a son, Jochi; Temujin and his family join the band of Jamuka; Temujin and Jamuka renew their vows of brotherhood and become *andas* for a third time.

1181   Temujin breaks with Jamuka.

1189   Temujin elected khan of less than half of the Mongols.

1190   Jamuka defeats Temujin.

1195   Torghil exiled to Qara Khitai; Temujin restores Torghil to his throne.

1196–   Temujin and Torghil help the Jurcheds to defeat the
1197   Tatars; Jurcheds reward Torghil with title of Ong (Wang) Khan; Temujin awarded minor title of *Ja'utquri* (keeper of the frontier).

1201   Mongol tribes elevate Jamuka to Gur-khan (supreme khan); Jamuka forms coalition against Temujin.

1202   Temujin exterminates the Tatars; Temujin and Ong Khan attack the Merkid tribe.

1203– Jamuka and others conspire against Temujin; Temujin
1204   retires to Lake Baljuna and swears to Baljuna Covenant; Temujin returns from Baljuna and defeats Ong Khan; death of Ong Khan; defeat of Tayang Khan and the Naimans; Temujin attacks the Merkid tribe.

1205   Death of Jamuka.

1206   Temujin invested with title of Genghis Khan at the Great Mongol *khuriltai* (council) and proclaimed leader of all people of the steppes.

1207   Genghis Khan invades the Tangut state of Hsi Hsia.

1209   Campaign against the Tanguts ends when the emperor of Hsi Hsia agrees to pay tribute to the Mongols; agreement leads to break between Hsi Hsia and Chin (Jurched) Empire.

1210   Genghis Khan refuses to pay tribute to Chin emperor.

1211   *Khuriltai* on Kerulen River; Mongols cross the Great Wall of China and launch campaign against Chin Empire.

1212   Genghis Khan wounded at Datong (Xijing) and withdraws to Inner Mongolia.

1213   Mongols resume campaign against the Chin.

1214   Siege of Zhongdu (Beijing); peace negotiated; Chin move capital to Kaifeng; Genghis Khan reopens campaign.

1215   Fall of Zhongdu.

1217   Genghis Khan commences campaign against Guchlug of Qara Khitai; Mongols sign trade treaty with Muhammad II, shah of Khwarizm.

1218   Jebe subdues Qara Khitans.

1219   Governor of northwestern province of Otrar in Khwarizm orders destruction of Mongol caravan and murder of Mongol ambassadors; Genghis Khan embarks on seven-year expedition to the West.

1220   Fall of Bukhara and Samarkand; Tolui demolishes Khorasan.

1221   Jebe and Subodei commence march around the Caspian Sea; Genghis Khan crosses the Hindu Kush and defeats Jalal al-Din on the banks of the Indus River.

1223   Jebe and Subodei ravage cities in Crimea and southern Russia.

1224   Jebe and Subodei rejoin Genghis Khan.

1225   Death of Jochi; Genghis Khan returns to Mongolia; Hsi Hsia and Chin Empire reestablish treaty relations.

1226   Mongols launch a further expedition against Hsi Hsia to break the Tangut alliance with the Chin; Genghis Khan injured in a fall from his horse.

1227   Death of Genghis Khan.

1234   Definitive conquest of Chin Empire.

1237   Batu extends Mongol conquests in Russia.

1241   Batu and Subodei invade Poland, Hungary, and Germany; death of Ogodei.

1242   Mongols under Batu and Subodei complete the conquest of Hungary and advance into Dalmatia, Croatia, and Austria; advance forces penetrate as far as Korneuburg and Weiner Neustadt, thirty miles south of Vienna; Batu discontinues campaign against western Europe upon learning of Ogodei's death.

Sources

CHAPTER ONE: Vast Lands, Scattered Peoples

p. 19, "The land is only . . ." Giovanni di Plano Carpini, *The Story of the Mongols Whom We Call the Tartars* (Translated by Erik Hildinger. Boston: Branden Publishing Company, 1996), 37.

p. 19, "The weather there is extremely variable . . ." Ibid.

p. 22-23, "They regard anything which can be eaten . . ." Ibid., 52.

p. 24, "Tartars are generally . . ." David Willis McCullough, ed., *Chronicles of the Barbarians: Firsthand Accounts of Pillage and Conquest, from the Ancient World to the Fall of Constantinople* (New York: History Book Club, 1998), 276.

p. 25, "The smallest are put on a cart . . ." Carpini, *Story of the Mongols*, 41.

p. 28, "[T]he stars turned . . ." Paul Ratchnevsky, *Genghis Khan: His Life and Legacy* (Translated and edited by Thomas Nivison Haining. Oxford, UK: Blackwell Publishers, 2002), 12.

CHAPTER TWO: Temujin

p. 34, "Her cap firmly on her head . . ." Ratchnevsky, *Genghis Khan*, 23.

p. 35, "Recently they took from us a lark . . ." Ibid.

p. 42-43, "In earlier days you swore . . ." Ibid., 33.

p. 43, "In gratitude for the black sable cloak . . ." Ibid.

CHAPTER THREE: A Heavenly Mandate

p. 47, "The Burkhan has . . ." Ratchnevsky, *Genghis Khan*, 34.

p. 49-50, "I have found my necessity . . ." Francis Woodman Cleaves, trans. and ed., *The Secret History of the Mongols: For the First Time Done in English out of the Original Tongue and Provided with an Exegetical Commentary* (Cambridge, MA: Harvard University Press, 1982), 45.

p. 51, "As a small child . . ." Ratchnevsky, *Genghis Khan*, 35.

p. 54, "The Prince [Temujin] dresses his people . . ." Ibid., 40.

p. 55, "Heaven and Earth have agreed . . ." Ibid., 41.

CHAPTER FOUR: Claiming the Title

p. 65, "We have not been loved . . ." Cleaves, *Secret History*, 70.

p. 66, "Couldn't you have spit it . . ." Jack Weatherford, *Genghis Khan and the Making of the Modern World* (New York: Crown Publishers, 2004), 49.

p. 66-67, "When we rout the enemy . . ." Ratchnevsky, *Genghis Khan*, 66.

p. 69, "When I have completed this great task . . ." Ibid., 72–73.

p. 75, "Let us be companions . . ." Weatherford, *Genghis Khan*, 63.

p. 75, "[W]hat use is there in my becoming a companion . . ." Ibid.

p. 75, "Kill me and lay down my dead bones . . ." Ibid., 64.

p. 76, "People of the Felt Walls," Ibid., 54.

CHAPTER FIVE: Right and Might

p. 77, "God spoke to me . . ." Ratchnevsky, *Genghis Khan*, 98.

p. 80, "punish the thieves . . ." Weatherford, *Genghis Khan*, 71.

p. 82-83, "If a troop commander is unable . . ." Ratchnevsky, *Genghis Khan*, 93.

p. 84, "If an ordinary regimental commander . . ." Ibid., 94.

p. 86-87, "Their cuirasses and horse armors . . ." Erik Hildinger, *Warriors of the Steppes: A Military History of Central Asia, 500 B.C. to 1700 A.D.* (Cambridge, MA: Da Capo Press,

2001), 120–21.

p. 87, "They wear defensive armor . . ." Ibid., 121.

CHAPTER SIX: A Promise on the Mountain
p. 91-92, "He was eager . . ." Ratchnevsky, *Genghis Khan*, 98.

p. 92, "You have never before allowed . . ." Ibid., 99.

p. 96, "If you, Genghis Khan, show me favor . . ." Ibid., 102.

p. 96, "bringing gold and silver . . ." Ibid.

p. 99, "We are a nation of town-dwellers . . ." Ibid., 105.

p. 101, "The Eternal Blue . . ." Weatherford, *Genghis Khan*, 84.

CHAPTER SEVEN: Across the Great Wall
p. 109, "[W]hen the Tartars see the enemy . . ." Carpini, *Story of the Mongols*, 75.

p. 113, "[I]f a place is well fortified . . ." Ibid., 76.

p. 113-114, "In their wars they kill . . ." Ibid., 78.

p. 117, "The siege was so . . ." Ratchnevsky, *Genghis Khan*, 113.

p. 117, "Your districts and counties . . ." Ibid.

p. 117-118, "took away from Zhongdu . . ." Ibid., 114.

p. 120, "When a few years later Baha . . ." Ibid., 115.

CHAPTER EIGHT: West of the Moon
p. 124, "I have the greatest desire . . ." Weatherford, *Genghis Khan,* 106.

p. 125-126, "henceforth the abscess of evil . . ." Ibid.

p. 126, "laid waste a . . ." Ibid.

p. 126, "The [shah] is no . . ." Ratchnevsky, *Genghis Khan*, 123.

p. 130, "I am the punishment . . ." Robert Marshall, *Storm from the East: From Genghis Khan to Khubilai Khan* (London: BBC Books, 1993), 53–54.

Bibliography

Archer, Christon I., John R. Ferris, Holger H. Herwig, and Timothy H. E. Travers. *World History of Warfare*. Lincoln: University of Nebraska Press, 2002.

Cantor, Norman. *The Civilization of the Middle Ages*. New York: HarperCollins Publishers, 1993.

Cantor, Norman, ed. *The Encyclopedia of the Middle Ages*. New York: Viking, 1999.

Carpini, Giovanni di Plano. *The Story of the Mongols Whom We Call the Tartars*. Translated by Erik Hildinger. Boston: Branden Publishing Company, 1996.

Cleaves, Francis Woodman, trans. and ed. *The Secret History of the Mongols*. Cambridge, MA: Harvard University Press, 1982.

Corvisier, André, ed. *A Dictionary of Military History*. English ed. Revised, expanded, and edited by John Childs. Translated by Chris Turner. Oxford, UK: Blackwell Publishers, 1994.

Cowley, Robert, and Geoffrey Parker, eds. *The Reader's Companion to Military History*. Boston: Houghton Mifflin, 1996.

Curtin, Jeremiah. *The Mongols: A History*. Conshohocken, PA: Combined Books, 1996.

Dahmus, Joseph. *A History of the Middle Ages*. New York: Barnes & Noble, 1995.

Daniels, Patricia, and Stephen G. Hyslop. *National Geographic*

Almanac of World History. Washington, DC: National Geographic, 2003.

Davies, Norman. *Europe: A History*. New York: Oxford University Press, 1996.

Dion, Frederic. *The Blue Wolf: The Epic Tale of the Life of Genghis Khan and the Empire of the Steppes*. Translated by Will Hobson. New York: St. Martin's Press, 2003.

Dupuy, R. Ernest, and Trevor N. Dupuy. *The Encyclopedia of Military History, from 3500 B.C. to the present*. Rev. ed. New York: Harper & Row, 1977.

Durant, Will. *The Story of Civilization*. Vol. 1, *Our Oriental Heritage*. New York: Simon & Schuster, 1963.

———. *The Story of Civilization*. Vol. 4, *The Age of Faith*. New York: Simon & Schuster, 1950.

Gibbon, Edward. *The Decline and Fall of the Roman Empire*. Vols. I and II. Great Books of the Western World, vols. 40 and 41. Chicago: Encyclopedia Britannica, 1952.

Hartog, Leo de. *Genghis Khan: Conqueror of the World*. New York: Barnes & Noble, 1999.

Hildinger, Erik. *Warriors of the Steppes: A Military History of Central Asia, 500 B.C. to 1700 A.D.* Cambridge, MA: Da Capo Press, 2001.

Holmes, Richard. *The Oxford Companion to Military History*. New York: Oxford University Press, 2001.

Hookham, Hilda. *A Short History of China*. New York: New American Library, 1972.

Hooper, Nicholas, and Matthew Bennett. *The Cambridge Illustrated Atlas of Warfare: The Middle Ages 768–1487*. New York: Cambridge University Press, 1996.

Humphrey, Judy. *Genghis Khan*. World Leaders Past & Present. Philadelphia: Chelsea House Publishers, 1987.

Kennedy, Hugh. *Mongols, Huns and Vikings: Nomads at War*. London: Cassell, 2002.

Kessler, Adam T. *Empires Beyond the Great Wall: The Heritage of Genghis Khan*. Los Angeles: Natural History Museum of Los Angeles County, 1993.

Kohn, George C. *A Dictionary of Wars*. New York: Facts On File, 1986.

Lamb, Harold. *Genghis Khan and the Mongol Horde*. New York: Random House, 1954.

———. *Genghis Khan: The Emperor of All Men*. New York: Robert M. McBride, 1928.

Langley, Andrew. *Genghis Khan and the Mongols*. Hove, East Sussex, UK: Wayland, 1987.

Legg, Stuart. *The Barbarians of Asia*. New York: Barnes & Noble, 1995.

Lister, R. P. *Genghis Khan*. New York: Barnes & Noble, 1993.

Lopez, Robert S. *The Birth of Europe*. New York: M. Evans, 1972.

Margiotta, Franklin D., ed. *Brassey's Encyclopedia of Land Forces and Warfare*. Washington, DC: Brassey's, 1996.

———. *Brassey's Encyclopedia of Military History and Biography*. Washington, DC: Brassey's, 1994.

Marshall, Robert. *Storm from the East: From Genghis Khan to Khubilai Khan*. London: BBC Books, 1993.

McCullough, David Willis, ed. *Chronicles of the Barbarians: Firsthand Accounts of Pillage and Conquest, from the Ancient World to the Fall of Constantinople*. New York: History Book Club, 1998.

Ratchnevsky, Paul. *Genghis Khan: His Life and Legacy*. Translated and edited by Thomas Nivison Haining. Oxford, UK: Blackwell Publishers, 2002.

Roux, Jean-Paul. *Genghis Khan and the Mongol Empire*. New York: Harry N. Abrams, 2003.

Seaton, Albert. *The Horsemen of the Steppes: The Story of the Cossacks*. New York: Barnes & Noble, 1996.

Spuler, Bertold. *History of the Mongols: Based on Eastern and*

Western Accounts of the Thirteenth and Fourteenth Centuries. Translated by Helga and Stuart Drummond. New York: Barnes & Noble, 1996.

Theisen, Gordon. *The Plunders of Genghis Khan*. New York: Lebhar-Friedman Books, 2001.

Turnbull, Stephen. *Genghis Khan & the Mongol Conquests 1190–1400*. Essential Histories series. London: Osprey Publishing, 2003.

———. *The Mongols*. Men-at-Arms Series. London: Osprey Publishing, 1995.

Weatherford, Jack. *Genghis Khan and the Making of the Modern World*. New York: Crown Publishers, 2004.

Wiencek, Henry, and Glen D. Lowry with Amanda Heller. *Storm Across Asia: Genghis Khan and the Mongols; The Mogul Expansion*. New York: HBJ Press, 1980.

Web sites

www.nationalgeographic.com/genghis
National Geographic's Web site for their special on Genghis Khan and his empire.

www.lacma.org/khan/index_flash.htm
A companion Web site to the Los Angeles County Museum of Art's exhibit on Genghis Khan and his legacy.

www.kiku.com/electric_samurai/virtual_mongol
A virtual guide to Mongolian culture.

www.thegreatwall.com.cn/en
History, tour, and pictures of the Great Wall of China.

Glossary

airak:	Fermented mare's milk; a mildly intoxicating beverage.
anda:	Sworn brother; blood brother.
arban:	A Mongol army unit of ten men.
Ba'atur:	A title meaning a powerful and noble warrior; strong prince; hero.
Baljuntu:	"Muddy Water Drinkers"; participants in the Baljuna Covenant.
Baljuna Covenant:	Oath of eternal allegiance sworn to Temujin at Lake Baljuna.
bilik:	Maxim; adage.
Borijin:	Name of Temujin's (Genghis Khan's) great clan.
Burkhan Khaldun:	Lit., "God Mountain"; located in the Hentiyn Nuruu (Khentii) range.
cangue:	A wooden collar, similar to an ox yoke, to which the hands of a prisoner were attached; used to control captives; also kan'g.
Four Coursers:	Boorchu, Boro'ul, Chila'un, and Mukali; the great generals whom Genghis Khan sent on important missions of great difficulty; a "courser," their namesake, is a swift or spirited horse.
Four Hounds:	Jebe, Jelme, Khubilai, and Subetai; favored lieutenants of Genghis Khan who spread terror and death among his enemies.
ger:	A round, portable tent made on a light wicker frame and covered in black felt.

gur-khan:	Supreme khan or king.
jagun:	A Mongol army unit of 100 men, or ten arbans.
keshig:	Elite guard; eventually numbering about 1,000 and serving as Genghis Khan's personal bodyguard.
khan:	A ruler, king, or chief.
khatun:	Wife of a ruler, king, or chief.
khuriltai:	An official council or meeting.
Kiyat:	Name of Temujin's (Genghis Khan's) minor clan; a split-off from the Borijin clan.
kotochin:	A member of a keshig household.
minghan:	A Mongol army unit of 1,000 men, or ten jaguns.
naadam:	Traditional Mongol games—horse racing, archery, and wrestling.
nerge:	Great annual hunt.
nokor:	Devoted follower.
ordu:	The court of a khan; camp; tent village.
Otchigen:	Lit., "prince of the hearth or fire"; suffix applied to the name of the youngest son in the family who traditionally inherits the father's estate.
shaman:	A magician-like priest.
sulde:	Spirit Banner: a spear with strands of horse hairs from the finest stallions tied to its shaft just below the blade; soul; spirit.
temur:	Iron.
tumen:	A Mongol regiment; the largest body of warriors acting as a unit, ranging in number from 500 men in Genghis Khan's early days to 10,000 men in his later days; ten minghans.
ulus:	A tribe; a nation.
Yasa:	Legal code of Genghis Khan.
Yeke Mongol Ulus:	Great Mongol Nation.
yurt:	An outsider's name for a ger; also yurta.

Index